50
psychology ideas
you really need to know

Adrian Furnham

Quercus

Contents

Introduction

Psychology has its advocates and detractors. Some think of it essentially as the 'queen of the social sciences' whose progress, insights and applications are keys to health, happiness and progress. Detractors see psychologists as deluded and even dangerous perpetrators either of commonsense or wrong ideas and practices.

The official birth of psychology was in the 1870s. Psychologists have been highly regarded international figures of influence. It could be argued that along with Darwin and Marx, Freud was the most influential thinker of the 19th century. Watson, Skinner, Milgram and others had a high impact on the way people do everything from raise and educate their children to how they select and manage people at work. And in the 21st century, a psychologist, for the second time, won the Nobel Prize for Economics.

Psychology is everywhere in today's society. No crime fiction, documentary, chat show, or medical consultation is complete without the introduction of a psychological angle. The design of your car, your house, your choice of clothes, consumables and partners, the way we teach our children – all have been the topic of, and influenced by, psychological research. It also has an accepted role in management, sports and consumer marketing.

Psychology is both a pure and applied science. It aims to understand behaviour and the basic mechanisms and processes that influence ideas, feelings and thoughts. It also tries to solve human problems. It is very multidisciplinary, having close connections with many other subjects including anatomy, medicine, psychiatry and sociology as well as economics, mathematics and zoology.

Newcomers to psychology are often surprised by the range of things that psychologists study – from dreaming to delusions of grandeur; computer phobia to the causes of cancer; memory to social mobility; attitude formation to alcoholism. Importantly and usefully, psychology teaches people a rich vocabulary through which they can describe and explain behaviour: psychology teaches the student the language of behavioural description and explanation.

Some psychological theories are counterintuitive and some are quite commonsensical. I hope that in this book I have made sense of the former and clarified the latter.

01 Abnormal behaviour

Abnormal psychology – also referred to as clinical psychology – is the study of abnormal behaviours. It looks at the origins, manifestations and treatments of disordered habits, thoughts or drives. These may be caused by environmental, cognitive, genetic or neurological factors.

Abnormal psychologists are concerned with the assessment, diagnosis and management of psychological problems. They are both scientists and practitioners who often specialize in the treatment of various disorders like anxiety disorders (anxiety, panic, phobias, post-traumatic stress disorders); mood disorders (depression, bipolar disorder, suicide); substance disorders (alcohol, stimulants, hallucinogens, etc.); or very complex problems like schizophrenia. Clinical psychology is part, but by no means the central part, of psychology. It is certainly associated by lay people as the most interesting and important specialism in applied psychology.

Defining abnormality While it is relatively easy to spot people who are distressed or acting bizarrely, it is much more difficult to define abnormality. 'Abnormal' means departure from the norm. So very tall and very short people are abnormal, as are very backward and very gifted people. Thus, strictly speaking, Einstein and Michelangelo were abnormal, as were Bach and Shakespeare.

For clinical psychology, the issue is not so much whether the behaviour is abnormal, as whether it is *maladaptive*, causing a person distress and social impairment. If a person's behaviour seems irrational or potentially harmful to themselves and others, we tend to think of that as abnormal. For the

timeline

1600	1773
First challenge to practice of witchcraft	First mental asylum built at Williamsburg, USA

psychologist it is called psychopathology; for the lay person, madness or insanity.

We would all like the certainty and clarity of a precise distinction between normal and abnormal. Yet we know that history and culture shape what is considered abnormal. Psychiatric textbooks reflect this. Homosexuality was not that long ago considered a mental illness. Masturbation in the 19th century was thought of as abnormal.

Socio-economic status, gender and race are all related to abnormality. Women are more likely to have anorexia, bulimia or anxiety disorders than men, who, in turn, are more likely to be substance abusers. Poor people are more likely to be diagnosed schizophrenic than rich people. American children suffer a high incidence of disorders of under-control compared to over-control, but that is the opposite way around in the West Indies.

Early approaches to abnormality saw bizarre behaviour as spirit possession. People believed in animalism – the belief that we are similar to animals – and that madness was the result of uncontrolled regression. Ancient Greeks saw abnormality and general malaise as caused by bodily fluids or 'humours'. As a result, early treatment of the insane was mostly involved in segregating them and then punishing them. Humane treatment didn't really appear until the 19th century.

Generally agreed-upon criteria Today, psychological definitions of abnormality revolve around a handful of generally agreed-upon criteria. These have been classified as the 4Ds: distress, deviance, dysfunction, danger. Abnormality generally involves *pain* and *suffering*, one aspect of which is acute and chronic personal suffering. One criterion is *poor adaptation* – not being able to do the everyday things of life, such as hold down a job, maintain happy interpersonal relationships or plan for the future.

A very common criterion is *irrationality* – bizarre, illogical beliefs about the physical or social world as well as, very often, the spiritual world.

'The years have layered onto this term (i.e. abnormal) too many value judgements and any number of synonyms are preferable: maladaptive, maladjusted, deviant, etc.'
A. Reber, 1985

1890s
Hypnosis, psychoanalysis starts

1940s
Behaviour therapies used

1952
First good diagnostic manual printed

Normality vs abnormality

Subjective This is perhaps the most primitive idea that uses ourselves, our behaviour, our values as the criteria of normality. This is the stuff of idiom and adage ('once a thief, always a thief'; 'there's nowt so queer as folk'). So people like us are normal, those different are not. This approach also tends to think in simple categories or non-overlapping types: normal–abnormal–very abnormal.

Normative This is the idea that there is an ideal, desirable state of how one should think and behave. This view of the perfect world is often developed by religious and political thinkers. Normality is perfection: the further from normality one is, the more abnormal. It's a more 'what ought to be' than 'what is reasonably possible' state of affairs. Nothing is normal because nobody is perfect.

Clinical Social scientists and medical clinicians attempt to assess the effectiveness, organization and adaptiveness of a person's functioning. Much depends on which dimension is being assessed. Clinicians also accept that the normal–abnormal distinctions are grey and somewhat subjective, though they strive for reliable diagnosis. Abnormality is usually associated with poor adaptations, pain or bizarre behaviours.

Cultural Culture dictates trends in everything from dress to demeanour, language to love. Culture prescribes and proscribes behaviours. Certain things are taboo, others are illegal. Again the further away or different from cultural norms a person appears to be, the more he or she is judged as abnormal. However, as cultural beliefs and practices change, so do definitions of normality. The case of homosexual behaviour nicely illustrates this issue.

Statistical All statisticians know the concept of the bell curve or the normal distribution. It has particular properties and is best known in the world of intelligence. Thus a score of 100 is average and 66 per cent of the population score between 85 and 115, and around 97 per cent between 70 and 130. Thus if you score below 70 and over 130 you are unusual, though the word 'abnormal' would not be applied. This model has drawbacks in the fact that behaviour that occurs frequently does not necessarily make it healthy or desirable. Also, while it may work for abilities which are reasonably straight-forward to measure, it works less easily with more subtle and multidimensional issues like personality or mental illness.

The behaviour of abnormal people is often incomprehensible to others. They are often unpredictable; they can be very volatile, changing from one extreme to another and often quite unable to control their behaviour. Their behaviour is often very inappropriate.

Almost by definition their abnormality is characterized by unconventional, usually rare, undesirable behaviours. In addition, abnormality has a moral dimension. It is associated with breaking rules, violating moral standards and disregarding social norms. Illegal, immoral, undesirable behaviour is abnormal.

One rather interesting criterion of abnormality is the discomfort that is generated in people around abnormal behaviour. Observers often feel uncomfortable around clear evidence of abnormality.

The problems of the concept The problems with any definition of abnormality are clear. Firstly, a healthy person in an unhealthy society is often labelled as abnormal. There are many examples where societies have been deeply intolerant of those who don't obey their narrow (unhealthy, maladaptive) standards of belief and behaviour. Secondly, of course, expert observers can't agree on the categorization of normal vs abnormal. Even when multiple criteria of abnormality are specified, there remains fundamental disagreement about whether a person is considered in some sense abnormal. Thirdly, there is the actor–observer difference: who is to make the judgement? Actors rarely think themselves abnormal: most of us are reasonably positive about ourselves and indeed have a great deal of information others do not have. Yet there are well-known traps and hazards in making a self-diagnosis. It is easier to be observers and label others abnormal, particularly those different from us or threatening to us.

> **She always says she dislikes the abnormal, it is so obvious. She says the normal is so much more simply complicated and interesting.**
>
> **G. Stein, 1935**

Self-diagnosis A primary goal of counselling, training and therapy is helping people become more self-aware. Clearly some mentally ill, and supposedly normal people, have little insight into their problems. They seem deluded. Equally students of abnormal psychology say they recognize that they have certain mental illnesses when they read textbooks. This occurs because many of us have an exaggerated sense of the uniqueness of some private, non-shared, even 'forbidden' or disapproved-of thoughts or behaviours. All of us hide certain aspects of ourselves and can suddenly see these alluded to in textbooks that list all sorts of abnormal behaviours.

the condensed idea
What is 'normal' behaviour?

02 Placebo effect

Doctors have been known to advise: 'Take two tablets and call me in the morning'. Although they know and acknowledge the idea that all (physical) treatments have active ingredients or procedures that produce physical changes in a patient, they know also of the power of psychological factors to cure all sorts of things. The concept of mind over matter in the world of health has been known for centuries.

What is it? 'Placebo' comes from the Latin word meaning 'to please'. A placebo is simply defined as a preparation with no medicinal value and no pharmacological effects. An active placebo is one that mimics the side-effects of the drug under investigation but lacks its specific, assumed therapeutic affect.

The sound of the flute will cure epilepsy and sciatic gout.
Theophrastus, 300 BC

Some believe placebo effects are more effective for psychological rather than physical illnesses. One important recent study showed that nearly 60 per cent of placebo-controlled patients did better than average waiting-list control patients, showing the power of the placebo.

History Modern research in the area is usually attributed to a paper written in the *American Dental Association Journal* over 50 years ago. Henry Beecher shocked the medical world by claiming that just placebo procedures like giving sugar pills or even sympathetically physically examining the patient would lead to an improvement in 30 per cent of patients. Today that estimate has increased to between a half to three-quarters of patients, with all sorts of problems from asthma to Parkinson's showing real lasting improvements from a range of treatments.

timeline

1500–1900	pre 20th century
Therapeutic properties ascribed to all sorts of substances	All medicine until modern times is the history of the placebo

Curing everything?

Placebos administered in an orthodox medical context have been shown to induce relief from symptoms in an impressively wide array of illnesses, including allergies, angina pectoris, asthma, cancer, cerebral infarction, depression, diabetes, enuresis, epilepsy, insomnia, Ménière's disease, migraine, multiple sclerosis, neurosis, ocular pathology, Parkinsonism, prostatic hyperplasia, schizophrenia, skin diseases, ulcers and warts.

Different placebos One question is: what type of placebo works best? The colour and size of capsules and pills have been repeatedly subject to experimental manipulation, but with little reliable impact. It does not seem to make much difference. One scientist reported that for a placebo to be maximally effective it should be very large and either brown or purple or very small and either bright red or yellow.

More serious, 'major' or invasive procedures do appear to have stronger placebo effects. Injections *per se* appear to have a greater impact than pills, and even placebo surgery (where people are cut open and sewn up with little or nothing done) has yielded high positive response rates.

The style of treatment administration and other qualities of the therapist appear to contribute substantially to the impact of the treatment itself. Those therapists who also exhibit greater interest in their patients, greater confidence in their treatments, and higher professional status, all appear to promote stronger placebo effects in their patients.

> **Kinship is healing: we are physicians to each other.**
> Oliver Sacks, 1973

1950s	1960s	1980s
First research into the placebo	Placebo controlled trials used	80 per cent of doctors still admit to using placebos

How do they work? The fascination with placebo effects has led to many ideas and theories as to how they actually work. All sorts of concepts have been proposed, including operant conditioning, classical conditioning, guilt reduction, transference, suggestion, persuasion, role demands, faith, hope, labelling, selective symptom monitoring, misattribution, cognitive dissonance reduction, control theory, anxiety reduction, expectancy effects and endorphin release.

Randomized, double-blind, control trials The placebo effect is both a blessing and a curse. It's a blessing for all therapists irrespective of what treatment they prescribe. It's a curse for scientists who try to evaluate the real effect of interventions. The placebo controlled, randomized, double-blind study has become the gold standard of scientific research to assess therapy and 'discount' any placebo effects.

> **It is the confession, not the priest that gives us absolution.**
>
> Oscar Wilde, 1890

The idea is that people are randomly sent to different groups, some of which are control groups having no treatment, alternative treatment or placebo treatment. Further, neither the doctor/scientist/therapist nor the client/patient knows which treatment they are receiving.

The first randomized, controlled trial took place soon after the Second World War. But it wasn't until 20 years ago that 'blinded' studies were introduced. It was recognized that because psychological factors may affect the response to treatment, the patient should be kept 'blind' to the nature of the treatment they got. Where both patient and clinician are unaware of the nature of the treatment (drug versus placebo, for instance), the trial is referred to as double-blind. Where the clinician is aware, but the patient is not, the trial is single-blind.

Problems Yet the placebo controlled, randomized, double-blind approach does have its difficulties. First, problems may arise because subjects randomized to different treatment groups may meet and discuss their treatment. Assignment to natural groups (e.g. comparison to two schools or two geographical regions) may be preferable to randomization. Next, blinding may not be feasible for some treatments. While neither doctor nor patient may be able to distinguish a real tablet from a sugar pill, placebo tablet, there are no clear equivalents to placebo drugs for some treatments. Third, participation in a study may affect the behaviour of people taking part. Simply being monitored and assessed regularly may in itself have a beneficial effect.

Fourth, participants agreeing to take part in a trial may not be typical of the general population of patients with that particular problem. Entry criteria to a trial need to be strict to ensure comparability between groups and to give the best chance of showing a treatment benefit. Another problem is the reduced compliance with treatment because of the possibility of receiving placebo treatment. If patients are told that they might be taking a placebo, they might be more inclined to give up on the treatment if there are no immediate effects.

'The best of healers is good cheer.'
Pindar, 500 BC

Sixth, using standard treatment in the trial may be artificial and have little relevance to the clinical practice. This may inhibit a more flexible patient-centred approach. The trial may therefore not be a true test of the therapy as used in clinical practice and the needs of the patient may conflict with the requirements of research. Next, individual variations in response are often ignored in an analysis that only considers average group responses. Patients who are made worse by the treatment may not be given enough attention in the reports, unless they suffered particularly obvious side-effects.

Eighth, ethical problems may arise in a variety of contexts, particularly where placebo treatments are involved or the patient or clinician has a marked preference for one treatment option over another. Ninth, the main outcome measure, based on clinical assessment and objective tests, may not reflect the patients' perspective of what constitutes an important and beneficial change. Patients may be more concerned with the quality of their lives, which may not be closely linked with changes in biochemical parameters or other disease indicators. Finally, the concern with eliminating the placebo effect when assessing a treatment in relation to a comparable placebo may mean that important psychological variables are neglected. Therapist characteristics and the attitude of the patient to treatment are seldom examined in a medical context, and yet may be important determinants to the patient's compliance with treatment and attitude toward illness.

'Medicine cures the man who is fated not to die.'
Proverb

the condensed idea
Susceptibility affects
treatment outcomes

03 Kicking the habit

'Every form of addiction is bad, no matter whether the narcotic be alcohol or morphine or idealism.' Carl Jung, 1960

Most people think of addictions primarily in terms of drugs. There is a long list of substances that people can and do become addicted to. These include alcohol, stimulants (like cocaine), opiates, hallucinogens, marijuana, tobacco and barbiturates.

Addiction involves the exposure to something and then the behaviour seeking to repeat the experience very often. Over time the addiction becomes established. There is regular and increasing consumption, with the takers knowing their habit is expensive, unhealthy and possibly illegal but seemingly being unable to give it up. It is a complex process that involves biological, psychological and social factors.

We drink to one another's health, and spoil our own.

Jerome K. Jerome, 1920

Some addiction researchers are interested in why some particular drugs or activities have such a propensity to become addictive. Others are fascinated by why some individuals seem more susceptible than others. Some scientists are concerned with the environmental and social conditions and features that make addictions more or less likely, while others look at attempts at recovery, and relapse from addiction.

Dependence vs abuse With regard to drugs, the psychiatric literature distinguishes between substance dependence and abuse. Both have technical meaning. *Dependence* has very specific characteristics like tolerance (people take more and more for limited effect); withdrawal symptoms (on not taking the drug); obsessions with trying to get hold of the drug; a

timeline

1875	1919–33
San Francisco bans opium	Prohibition in USA

Smoking

The two most discussed addictions are cigarette smoking and alcohol consumption. In most Western countries around a quarter to a third of people still smoke, and smoking is thought to cause a third of all cancers. Smoking is now a 'stigmatized habit' which has many causes. The factors that lead a person to start smoking (social pressure, role models) are often different from those that cause them to continue. Nicotine is a powerful stimulant: it increases heart rate and blood pressure; it decreases body temperature; it changes hormones released by the pituitary gland, and it releases adrenalin. The release of dopamine in the brain makes it reinforcingly addictive. More importantly, people continue because of the unpleasant withdrawal symptoms that occur – anxiety, headaches, irritability and insomnia. Quitting smoking has immediate and long-term effects.

Many individuals try to reduce and give up smoking. Governments use advertising bans, restrictive sales and consumption sites and price increases, with modest effects, as well as health and education campaigns. Individuals try everything from nicotine replacement patches and gum; psychotherapy and hypnotism; and finally just plain willpower. Because many factors – visual, olfactory, physiological and social – trigger the need for a cigarette, many smokers find it impossible to kick the habit.

deterioration in all social, occupational and recreational activities; and continued use with full knowledge of all the damage that is being done.

Abuse means using the drug despite the need to fulfil various school, home and work obligations; use in dangerous situations (driving, at work); use despite illegal behaviour; use despite persistent negative side-effects.

The addictive personality The original idea was that people had some particular profile or flaw or vulnerability that made them prone to specific or all addictions. However, the concept has not been successful. Some psychiatrists see addiction as a consequence of mental illness like depression or anti-social personality disorder. The idea is that risk-takers or the mentally ill are vulnerable to becoming reliant on drug taking as a crutch. They are more likely to experiment and ignore or downplay any potentially adverse consequences.

1935	1960s	2000s
Founding of Alcoholics Anonymous	Counter-culture advocates psycho-active drugs	Widespread bans on smoking in public places

Psychiatric criteria for substance dependence

A maladaptive pattern of substance use, leading to impairment or distress, as manifested by many of the following, occurring at any time in the same 12-month period.

1. Tolerance, meaning either a need for markedly increased amounts of the substance to achieve intoxication or desired effect and/or markedly diminished effect with continued use of the same amount of the substance.

2. Withdrawal showing as withdrawal syndrome for the specific substance or where the same (or a closely related) substance is taken to relieve or avoid withdrawal symptoms.

3. The substance is often taken in larger amounts or over a longer period than was intended.

4. A persistent desire or unsuccessful efforts to cut down or control substance use.

5. Much of the time is spent in activities necessary to obtain the substance, or recover from its effects.

6. Important social, family, occupation or leisure activities are given up or reduced because of substance use.

7. Substance use is continued despite clear knowledge of having a persistent or recurrent physical or psychological problem that is likely to have been caused or exacerbated by the substance.

Therapists also point out how addicts and drug-dependent people use drugs to compensate or cope. Drugs are used to numb feelings, reduce painful emotional states or reduce internal conflict. It may help loneliness or make up for a lack of gratifying relationships with others. Drug takers feel they can only say and do things when under the influence of the drugs and therefore, in time, they become dependent on the specific drugs for effective social functioning.

Genetic vulnerability Addictions run in families. Thus the children of alcoholics are four times more likely themselves to be alcoholic than children of non-alcoholics. Twin studies have clearly indicated that substance abuse has genetic determinants. It is likely that complex genetic factors lead to an individual's particular biological response to drugs, probably specifically around neurotransmitter systems. So people may be self-medicating with drugs that 'correct for' a biochemical imbalance in the brain that they have inherited.

'**Drunkenness is simply voluntary insanity.**'

Seneca, **60 BC**

Opponent-process theory This theory states that systems react and adapt to stimuli by opposing their initial effects. A desire, then craving, for something which did not exist before any experience of the drug, increases with exposure to it. A number of phenomena are associated with all addiction and dependence. The first is *affective pleasure* – a physical and emotional hedonic state that follows use. It could be relaxation, or stress release, or just feelings of sudden energy. Then there is *affective tolerance*, which means that one needs more and more of the substance to have the same effect. The third, is *affective withdrawal*, which is what occurs if the drug is not taken.

So the drug causes a process which sets off an opposite reaction which grows in strength with repeated exposure. This is *affective contrast*. With more use, the dominant reaction is negative. So one needs the drug to achieve a neutral state and little pleasure is derived from taking the drug.

Positive-reinforcement theory Drugs can make one feel good, even euphoric. In the 1960s psychologists allowed monkeys to 'self-administer' morphine and they showed all signs of addiction. Psychologists have become increasingly interested in the drug reward pathways in the brain, particularly the brain regions and neurotransmitters that may be involved in 'natural rewards' like food and sex versus artificial stimulants like drugs and electrical brain stimulation. We know that drugs like cocaine and amphetamines increase synaptic dopamine in the brain region called the nucleus accumbens. So lots of drugs give us real highs that we want to repeat.

> **Cocaine isn't habit-forming. I should know – I've been using it for years.**
> **Tallulah Bankhead, 1960**

Learning theories Drug-taking and the pleasures associated with it become associated with very specific situations, sights and sounds. Thus people associate the drugs from alcohol to amphetamines with very specific cues or reminders. Put people in particular settings and they will experience drug cravings – so pubs for alcoholics or the smell of smoke for nicotine addicts, induce cravings. Cues that deliver impending drug delivery can induce strong desires which 'have to be' fulfilled. In many senses this is the old-fashioned behaviourism and conditioning theory.

the condensed idea
The mind causes and cures addiction

04 Lost touch

Most people are terrified by the prospect of meeting a schizophrenic. They are thought of as deranged, dangerous and demented as well as unhinged, unpredictable and uncontrollable. Films and books have probably done more to perpetuate myths about this condition than to explain it. Schizophrenia is a psychotic illness characterized by a disorder of thoughts and perceptions, behaviours and moods.

Incidence Schizophrenia affects 1 in 100 people and is the most serious of mental disorders. Roughly a third of people require long-term institutionalization; a third show remission and could be considered cured; while a third have periods of symptoms followed by 'normality'. They are different because of the symptoms that they do have (positive) and don't have (negative) compared with normal people. They tend to have various manifestations of thought disorders (disorganized, irrational thinking), delusions and hallucinations. They tend to lack energy, initiative and social contacts. They are emotionally very flat, have few pleasures and are withdrawn.

> ‘Schizophrenia cannot be understood without understanding despair.’
>
> R.D. Laing, 1955

Schizophrenia often has major social and occupational consequences. 'Episodes' can last for long periods of time and reoccur. It is for many, but not all, a debilitating and long-lasting problem.

History and misconceptions There are many common misconceptions about schizophrenics. The first is that they are dangerous, uncontrollable and unpredictable, while the reality is that most are rather shy, withdrawn and concerned with their problems. The second is that they have a split Jekyll and Hyde personality, whereas what is split is the emotional

timeline

1893	1908
Kraepelin describes schizophrenia	Bleuler first uses the term 'schizophrenia'

(affective) and cognitive (thought) aspect. Third, many people believe they do not, and cannot, recover and that once a schizophrenic always a schizophrenic.

It was not until the turn of the 20th century that Emil Kraepelin, a German psychiatrist, tried to draw up the first psychiatric classification system. One disorder he called *dementia praecox*, which meant predictive deterioration, and he described various behavioural cues that we today would call schizophrenia. He influenced many in the field in his belief that the cause and therefore 'cure' would be biomedical. Another German, Adolph Meyer, argued at the beginning of the 20th century that there was no physiological basis to the disease and that it originated from early learning problems and underdeveloped interpersonal processes.

Classification The classification of schizophrenia remains complex because of the diversity of symptoms. These include delusions; hallucinations; disorganized speech (incoherence, loose association, use of nonsense words); disorganized behaviour (dress, body posture, personal hygiene); negative, flat emotions; poor insight into their problems; and depression.

Because of complications with the diagnosis, various subtypes have been named. Thus there is *paranoid* and *catatonic* schizophrenia. Catatonics (from the Greek 'to stretch or draw tight') often adopt odd, stationary poses for long periods of time. Paranoid schizophrenics have delusions of control, grandeur and persecution and are consistently suspicious of all around them. *Disorganized* schizophrenics manifest bizarre thoughts and language, with sudden inappropriate emotional outbursts. Some psychiatrists mention *simple* or *undifferentiated* schizophrenia. Others have distinguished between *acute* (sudden, severe onset) and *chronic* (prolonged, gradual onset). Another distinction is between Type I (mostly positive symptoms) and Type II (mostly negative symptoms).

Conceptual dispute

The diagnostic term 'schizophrenia' is a major cause of dispute and debate among psychiatrists, patient groups and the lay public. The most common objection is that it is an unhelpful umbrella term that covers a range of different disorders with different symptoms and different causes. Diagnosis is therefore unreliable. Some advocate the idea of *schizotypy*, which refers to a continuum of personality characteristics and experiences related to psychoses, particularly schizophrenia. This is different from the categorical view that you either have or do not have the problem.

1933
T.S. Eliot talks of 'split personality'

1946
MIND: mental health charity founded

1950s
Development of effective antipsychotic drugs

> **Psychophrenia: a successful attempt not to adapt to pseudo-social realities.**
>
> R.D. Laing, 1958

There is still no complete agreement about the subtypes or the precise 'deficits' in functioning, though these usually come under four headings: cognitive or thinking; perceptual or seeing; motor or moving; emotional or feeling. Researchers are continuing to seek out the source or cause of areas of 'vulnerability' that cause some people to develop schizophrenia. So there are increasingly sophisticated genetic studies as well as those looking particularly at complications of pregnancy and traumatic childhood experiences, brain functioning and family and cultural influences.

Researchers as well as medical and lay people tend to believe in, or follow, different approaches that describe the cause and cure of schizophrenia. Essentially these split into biological models, stressing genetic, biochemical or brain structure causes; and the socio-psychological, focusing on problems of communication and punishment in early life. Certainly developments in behavioural genetics and brain science have led to more interest in the biological approach to cause and cure.

The medical model In this model schizophrenic persons are in most cases called 'patients', reside in 'hospitals', and are 'diagnosed', given a 'prognosis' and then 'treated'. The medical model regards mental mal-function such as that found in the schizophrenic patient primarily as a consequence of physical and chemical changes, primarily in the brain. Twin and adoption studies have convinced most researchers that a genetic factor is involved. Other researchers have concentrated on brain biochemistry. Some hypothesize the existence in schizophrenics of brain abnormalities, possibly caused by a virus. Treatment consists primarily of medical and sometimes surgical procedures, but mainly the use of neuroleptic (antipsychotic) drugs.

The moral-behavioural model Schizophrenics according to this model are seen as suffering for their 'sinful' or problematic behaviour in the past. Much schizophrenic behaviour contravenes moral or legal principles, and this is the key to both understanding and curing the disorder. Treatment is by far the most important aspect of the moral-behavioural model, which is rarely held in developed countries these days. Whether behaviour is seen as sinful, irresponsible, simply maladjusted or socially deviant, the crucial thing is to change it so as to make it socially acceptable. The methods used range from simple moral exhortations to complex behavioural techniques, such as token economies – a form of behaviour modification, verbal control of behaviour, and social-skills training.

The psychoanalytic model The psychoanalytic model differs from the others in that it is interpretative, treating the patient as an agent capable of meaningful action. Rather than seeing people with schizophrenia as 'acted on' by various forces (both biological and environmental) that cause them to behave in certain ways, the psychoanalytic conception is concerned with patients' intentions, motives and reasons. This model suggests that unusual or traumatic early experiences or the failure to negotiate some critical stage of emotional development are the primary causes of schizophrenia. The behaviour of the person with schizophrenia is to be interpreted symbolically; it is the therapist's task to decode it. Long-term, one-to-one therapy with a trained psychoanalyst is the primary treatment offered by this model.

> ‘It is hypothesised that a person caught in a double bind may develop schizophrenic symptoms.’
>
> **G. Bateson, 1956**

The social model In this model, mental illness is seen partly as a symptom of a 'sick' society (others being a high divorce rate, work pressures, juvenile delinquency, increased drug addiction). The pressures of the modern world fall more heavily on the poor and disadvantaged, and thus they seem to suffer more of what is described as 'illness'. There is no individual treatment in the social model. Instead what is required is large-scale social change to reduce the stresses on individuals and thus the incidence of mental illness.

The conspiratorial model The conspiratorial theory is perhaps the most radical conceptual model of schizophrenia in that it denies the existence of mental illness (as a physical disorder) and stands in direct opposition to the medical model. Mental illness is not 'something someone has', but 'something someone does or is'. Psychiatric diagnoses are, according to this model, simply stigmatizing labels applied to persons whose behaviour offends or annoys others, and are used to control eccentric, radical or politically harmful activity.

the condensed idea
The concept of
schizophrenia has evolved

05 Not neurotic, just different

'Our whole life is taken up with anxiety for personal security, with preparations for living, so that we really never live at all.'
Leo Tolstoy, 1900

There have long been those who challenge the power, practices and pretensions of psychiatrists. Critics, dissidents and reformers have at different times and in different countries made stinging attacks on conventional academic and biological psychiatry.

Politics and psychiatry Inevitably as psychiatry became more established and institutionalized as a medical practice, it had its detractors who liked neither psychiatrists' power nor their labels. There are the various accounts from artists and writers as well as patient groups who strongly opposed particular treatments (drugs, electroshock and surgery) for various 'mental' diseases. There were famous cases from Nazi Germany and Soviet Russia that illustrated how psychiatry was used as an oppressive political force. Psychiatrists seem in some situations to operate as part of the repressive arm of the state.

Anti-psychiatry critics questioned three things: the medicalization of madness; the existence of mental illness; and the power of psychiatrists to diagnose and treat certain individuals with compulsion. Anti-psychiatry was more than anti-custodial: it was often anti-state, almost anarchic. It saw many state institutions, particularly mental hospitals, as distorting and repressing the human spirit and potential in various groups.

It was not until the 1960s that the term 'anti-psychiatry' came into use. There were a number of different strands to the various groups that formed

timeline

1960
Szasz, *The Myth of Mental Illness*

1961
Goffman, *Asylums*

together under this umbrella term. And paradoxically perhaps, the greatest critics were psychiatrists themselves.

History of the movement There were three main origins of the movement. The first started in the early 1950s and was a result of the war between Freudian-inspired psychoanalytic psychiatrists and the new biological-physical psychiatrists. The former, who were losing power and who favoured protracted, dynamic, talking cures, were challenged by the latter, who saw that approach as not only costly and ineffective but profoundly unscientific. The biological psychological treatments were surgical and pharmacological and they had some important early successes. The old guard challenged the new guard.

The second attack began in the 1960s with figures like David Cooper, R.D. Laing and Thomas Szasz in different countries getting highly vocal about the use of psychiatry to control those deviating from societal norms. Thus

Being sane in an insane place

One of the most famous anti-psychiatry studies was done in the early 1970s. Eight 'normal', mentally healthy researchers tried to gain admission, through diagnosis, to a number of American mental hospitals. The only symptom they reported was hearing voices. Seven were diagnosed as schizophrenic and admitted. Once in the hospital they behaved normally and were ignored when they politely asked for information. They later reported that their diagnostic label of schizophrenia meant they had low status and power in the hospital.

Then they 'came clean' and admitted they had no symptoms and felt fine. But it took nearly three weeks before they were discharged, often with the diagnosis 'schizophrenia in remission'. So normal, healthy people could easily be diagnosable as 'abnormal'. But could the reverse happen? The same researchers told psychiatric hospital staff that fake or pseudo-patients pretending to be schizophrenics may try to gain access to their hospital. They then found that 19 genuine patients were suspected as frauds by two or more members of staff, including a psychiatrist.

The conclusion was that it is not possible to distinguish the sane from the insane in mental hospitals. Though this famous study has received considerable criticism on ethical and experimental grounds, it added great impetus to the anti-psychiatry movement.

1967	1980s onwards	2000
Cooper, *Psychiatry and Anti-psychiatry*	Extensive closure of mental hospitals	Widespread critique of drug companies

people who were seen to be sexually, politically or morally deviant or different were subject to psychiatric processing and control. Szasz's famous book *The Myth of Mental Illness* explains this position well.

The third force were American and European sociologists, notably Erving Goffman and Michel Foucault, who saw the devious power of psychiatry and its effects on labelling, stigmatizing and hospitalizing people.

The high point of this movement occurred at the time of the 1960s counter-cultural, challenging spirit of the age. Popular films (like *One Flew Over the Cuckoo's Nest*) and radical magazines appeared that challenged the biological psychiatrists, state services and practices.

The anti-psychiatry movement was always a loose coalition between social action groups and they tended to focus on very specific problems like schizophrenia or the sexual disorders. They talked of authenticity and liberation, of empowerment and personal management rather than pharmaceutical intervention. Many began to attack the pharmaceutical industry and the established institutions like the Victorian mental hospitals.

Fundamental beliefs The movement did share some fundamental beliefs and concerns. The first was that families, institutions and the state are as much a cause of illness as a person's biological functioning or genetic make-up. Second, they opposed the medical model of illness and treatment. They believed that those who were living by different codes of conduct were erroneously and dangerously labelled delusional. Third, they believed that certain religious and ethnic groups were oppressed because they were in some sense abnormal. They were pathologized and therefore made to believe they needed treatment.

The movement was very concerned with the power of diagnostic labels. They saw those labels as giving a bogus impression of accuracy and immutability. Diagnostic labels and manuals are rejected because people meet multiple criteria (or none) and there is little agreement between experts.

> **Neurosis is always a substitute for legitimate suffering.**
>
> Carl Jung, 1951

Attacks on therapy The movement also focused its opposition on very specific therapies, particularly drugs such as those designed to treat primarily childhood problems (ADHD) and depression. They attacked them because of their costs and side-effects and also because patients were not told the truth about them. Anti-psychiatry activists have focused on all aspects of pharmaceutical company behaviour, arguing that they fake their data and massively overcharge for their drugs. This in turn has led the industry to be carefully monitored and policed by legislative actions.

Other targets have been electro-convulsive therapy (ECT) as well as very specific procedures like brain surgery (prefrontal lobotomies). Despite certain evidence of success, critics argue they are 'forced upon' naïve patients and cause massive permanent side-effects.

The power of psychiatrists to section or involuntarily hospitalize patients is also attacked by the movement. Many critics see professional psychiatrists as an arm of the state, and on a par with policemen, judges and juries.

Anti-psychiatry advocates called for a more humane psychiatry. They still challenge psychiatric language and the illusion of a biomedical, scientific psychiatry that searches for biological and genetic explanations. Thus, for instance, they are saying that poverty, not neurotransmitter dysfunction, is the major cause of depression.

The original movements were ideologically based, heavily politicized, anti-reductionists. They attempted to exorcize and rehabilitate psychiatry. They opposed 'the system'. In many ways they succeeded: many treatments have been stopped; many mental hospitals closed. Psychiatric labels have changed and are used with much more care.

The anti-psychiatry movement has transformed into the patient-based consumer movement. The focus is not so much on trying to dismantle organized psychiatry but rather on patients' rights and power.

The new psychiatry

Many psychiatrists have attempted to answer the anti-psychiatry critics by adopting specific principles or guidelines. Thus they may try to institute the following.

Firstly, admit that the goal of treatment is to get better rather than just increase insight or self-understanding. Secondly, treatment should be evidence-based and only proven treatments used. Thirdly, recognize that patients have the right to see their files, know their diagnosis, be told about what treatments are available and their associated risks. Patients and psychiatrists should have realistic expectations of what treatment and therapy can and cannot do. All patients with psychiatric illnesses deserve care, compassion and respect.

the condensed idea
Psychiatry has its critics

06 Seem sane

'Psychopaths are without conscience and incapable of empathy, guilt or loyalty to anyone but themselves.'
Paul Babiak and Robert Hare, 2006

Subtle differences Controversy surrounds the concept of the psychopath ('psychopathic personality' and 'sociopath' are sometimes used synonymously). Psychopathy is a personality disorder characterized by people who have no conscience and are incapable of empathy, guilt or loyalty to anyone but themselves. Sociopathy is a non-psychiatric condition and refers to those who are anti-social and criminal and follow the norms of a particular subculture. 'Anti-social personality disorder' is a broad category that embraces both conditions.

Some believe diagnosing or calling someone a psychopath is vague, contradictory and used by psychiatrists as a catch-all category for people too difficult or dangerous to diagnose. However, the condition has become well known since the book by H. Cleckley (1941) called *The Mask of Sanity*.

Egocentrism and lies Being a psychopath affects every aspect of a person's life. Overall psychopaths tend to be impulsive and irresponsible, with few clear life goals. They have a history of problems with authority and poor behavioural controls. They lack empathy and remorse and never accept responsibility for their actions.

> **Psychopaths couldn't care less about the feelings of others or rules of society. Where others seek to build, they destroy.**
> Oldham and Morris, 1995

They have been called hollow – their relationships are superficial and they have no loyalty to anyone except themselves. They have little sense of who they are and have no value system or long-range goals. Most of all, they cannot 'bide time'. They like the here and now, and an exciting one at that. They eschew stability and routine. Further, they often seem devoid of social or physical anxiety.

timeline

1900s	1941
First idea of mad and bad, not just bad	Cleckley, *The Mask of Sanity*

Diagnostic criteria

1. Psychopaths show a disregard for, and violation of, the rights of others. They often have a history of being difficult, delinquent or dangerous.

2. They fail to conform to social norms with respect to lawful behaviours (repeatedly performing acts that are grounds for arrest, imprisonment and serious detention). This includes, lying, stealing and cheating.

3. They are always deceitful, as indicated by repeated lying, use of aliases, or conning others for personal profit or pleasure. They are nasty, aggressive, con artists – the sort who often get profiled on business crime programmes.

4. They are massively impulsive and fail to plan ahead. They live only in, and for, the present.

5. They show irritability and aggressiveness, as indicated by repeated physical fights or assaults. They can't seem to keep still – ever.

6. They manifest a reckless disregard for the physical and psychological safety of others.

7. They are consistently irresponsible. Repeated failure to sustain consistent work behaviour or to honour financial obligations are their hallmark.

8. They show a lack of remorse. They are indifferent to, or rationalize, having hurt, mistreated or stolen from another. They never learn from their mistakes. It can seem that labelling them as anti-social is a serious understatement.

Psychopaths are nearly always in trouble with the law and authority figures. What gets them into trouble is impulsiveness. They are not planners and think little about either the victim of their crime or the consequences for themselves. Their crimes are frequently petty, deceitful thefts but are most often fraud, forgery and failure to pay debts.

The first response to being found out is to escape, leaving colleagues, family or debtors to pick up the pieces. They do so without a qualm. The next response is to lie with apparent candour and sincerity even under oath and even to parents and loved ones. They behave as if social rules and

1960s	1964	2006
First diagnostic criteria/checklist developed	McCord, *The Psychopath: An Essay on the Criminal Mind*	Babiak and Hare, *Snakes in Suits: When the Psychopath Goes To Work*

regulations do not really apply to them. They have no respect for authorities and institutions, families and traditions.

Psychopaths are at the mercy of their impulses. Whereas neurotics tend to be over-controlled, the psychopath shows inadequate control. They are childlike in their demands for immediate total gratification. They also seek thrills, often associated with alcohol, drugs, gambling and sex.

Superficiality Clever, handsome psychopaths have massive but superficial charm. They have to keep 'on the move' because they get to be known in the community. Their geographic and vocational mobility is indeed a good index of their pathology. They have to make up stories of their past.

Curiously, when asked about justice and morality in the abstract, they tend to give 'correct' conventional answers. They just don't apply this knowledge of right and wrong to themselves. This is particularly the case when their judgement conflicts with their personal demands for immediate gratification.

Unempathic Psychopaths have inevitably problematic relationships. They seem incapable of love and deep friendship for several reasons. They manifest a near complete absence of empathy, gratefulness and altruism. They are selfish, not self-sacrificial. Most crucially they appear not to understand others' emotions. They seem completely ungrateful for the help and affection of others. Other people are seen as a source of gain and pleasure irrespective of their discomfort, disappointment or pain. Others' needs are too trivial.

Vanity and lack of empathy mean the psychopath finds it difficult to predict how others will behave and which of his or her own many behaviours will lead to punishment. Psychopaths are in essence completely amoral. They accept no responsibility for their actions and therefore no blame, guilt, shame or remorse. They are able to mouth trite excuses and rationalizations for the benefit of others. Indeed they often have a convincing façade of competence and maturity. They can appear attentive, charming, mature and reliable – but have difficulty maintaining the façade. They can do so long enough to get a job or even get married but not to sustain either.

> **Psychopaths usually don't get along well with one another. The last thing an egocentric, selfish, demanding, callous person wants is someone like him.**
>
> **Robert Hare, 1999**

Psychopaths at work The first question is why they are attracted to certain jobs and they to them. They seem attracted to entrepreneurial, start-up business or those in the process of radical change such as when removing layers of management. It is when businesses are chaotic that they are often at their best.

Psychopaths at work are often called 'normal' or industrial, or even 'successful' psychopaths because they appear to be relatively normal and successful at work. They succeed for various reasons but tend to adopt strategies that lead them to cope. They build up a network of one-to-one relationships with powerful, useful and influential people. They find out how various people can help them, exploit them and then cast them aside irrespective of the promises they have made.

They avoid group/committee meetings because they say very different things to different people and can't present a single façade or voice that is coherent. Co-workers, colleagues and reports are frequently abandoned when their usefulness is at an end. They deliberately create conflict between individuals to try to prevent them sharing information about them. All detractors are 'neutralized' not so much by violence or threats but by raising doubts about their integrity and loyalty as well as their competence. Psychopaths seek out organizations in flux or change as well as those with poor monitoring systems so that they are rarely threatened or challenged.

Treatment Experts are divided on what sort of treatment to offer and whether it works to teach compassion, planning and honesty. Some talk of management rather than cure. Some have argued that CBT works; others of incarceration of the most dangerous in secure hospitals.

There are various books that mention being careful, documenting issues and being aware of the many tricks of the psychopath. They are clearly most dangerous if they are attractive, clever and well educated. No wonder movie directors seem to choose this mental disorder above all others in thrillers.

the condensed idea
Psychopaths wear a mask of sanity

07 Stress

The word 'stress' is derived from the Latin *stringere*, which means 'to draw tight'. Many definitions exist: some believe stress can and should be subjectively defined (what I say about how I feel); others feel one needs an objective definition (perhaps physical measures of saliva, blood or heart beat). Some researchers believe a global definition is appropriate (there is one general thing called stress); others emphasize that stress is multidimensional (it is made up of many different features).

Historic trends

Until the 18th century, 'stress' colloquially implied hardship, adversity or affliction (specific types of stress). It was later used by physicists to describe a force exerted upon an object, so that resultant changes in volume, shape and size were called 'strains'. Hence, stresses and strains.

In the 19th century, the pursuit and maintenance of a constant internal state was seen as the essence of 'free and independent life'. This motivation towards equilibrium was called 'homeostasis', from the Greek words

homoios meaning 'similar' and *stasis* meaning 'state'. Stress was considered to be a threat to homeostasis (a 'rocking of the boat').

By the mid-1950s researchers seemed to have settled on the response-based definition of stress as 'the sum of all non-specific changes caused by function or damage'. This was later reworded to 'the non-specific response of the body to any demand made upon it', rendering it even more inclusive.

timeline

1946	1964
Han Selye's first definition of stress	Type A, stress and heart disease

Should you define stress by the outside stimulus factors that cause it or rather how people respond to it? That is, if somebody does not experience something as stressful, can we really call it a stressor?

Demands and control

Various models or theories try to describe and understand stress. The simplest is the demand–control theory, which looks at the various psychological and physical demands put on the person to behave in a particular way and the control or decision latitude they have in delivering them. High-demand, low-control situations are worst. Another way of describing this is challenge and support.

Three components

Firstly, stress can be a function of the make-up of the individual, particularly their personality, ability and biography. Secondly, there are features about the environment (job, family, organization), usually but not exclusively considered in terms of the work environment. Thirdly, there is how the individual and the environment perceive, define but more importantly try to cope with stress, strains and pressures.

The individual

Firstly there are the anxious worriers (sometimes called neurotics). People with 'negative affectivity', a mix of anxiety, irritability, neuroticism and self-deprecation, tend to be less productive, less job-satisfied and more prone to absenteeism.

Challenge and support at work

Much support, little challenge People in this situation are in the fortunate position of good technical and social support, but the fact they are under-challenged probably means that they underperform. They may actually be stressed by boredom and monotony.

Much support, much challenge This combination tends to get the most out of people as they are challenged by superiors, subordinates, shareholders and customers to 'work smarter' but are given the appropriate support to succeed.

Little support, much challenge This unfortunate, but very common, situation is a major cause of stress for any manager because he or she is challenged to work consistently hard but only offered minimal emotional, informational (feedback) and physical (equipment) support.

Little support, little challenge People in some bureaucracies lead a quiet and unstressed life because they are neither challenged nor supported, which usually means neither they nor their organization benefit.

1980	1990	2000s
Concept of burnout introduced	Post-traumatic stress disorder widely researched	Stress at work widely cited in court cases

❝Stress has become a trivial concept without a clear set of physical symptoms.❞

R. Briner, 2001

Secondly there are fatalists. People who believe that the events that occur in their lives are the result of their own behaviour and/or ability, personality and effort have less stress than those who believe events in their lives to be a function of luck, chance, fate, God, powerful others or powers beyond their control.

Thirdly there are the competitive, frantic people with competitive drive and an enhanced sense of time urgency. These people have an intense sustained desire to achieve, an eagerness to compete, persistent drive for recognition, a continuous involvement in deadline activities, a habitual propensity to accelerate mental and physical functions, and consistent alertness.

The job (organization) or social environment Some jobs are more stressful than others. The greater the extent to which the job requires making decisions, constant monitoring of machines or materials, repeated exchange of information with others, unpleasant physical conditions, and performing unstructured rather than structured tasks, the more stressful the job tends to be.

Some people have to engage in role-juggling – rapidly switching from one role and one type of activity to another (from boss to friend, teacher to partner, law enforcer to father confessor). Role ambiguity can occur when people are uncertain of the scope of their responsibilities, what is expected of them, and how to divide their time between various duties.

Over- and under-load stress result from having too little, or too much, to do. Many people are (or should be) responsible for their subordinates: they have to motivate them, reward and punish them, communicate and listen to them, and so on. Being socially isolated or ignored is another source of stress. Having friends and supporters in times of difficulty helps managers see stressful events as less threatening and more controllable than if they had little or no support. Lack of participation in decisions produces a sense of helplessness and alienation.

Coping One distinction that has been made is between *problem-focused coping* (aimed at problem-solving or doing something to alter the source of stress) and *emotion-focused coping* (aimed at reducing or managing the emotional distress that is associated with, or cued by, a particular set of circumstances). Emotion-focused responses can involve denial; others involve positive reinterpretation of events; and still others involve the seeking out of social support. Similarly, problem-focused coping can potentially involve several distinct activities, such as planning, taking direct action, seeking assistance, screening out particular activities, and sometimes stopping acting for an extended period.

Optimism: a buffer against stress Optimists are hopeful in their outlook on life, interpret a wide range of situations in a positive light, and tend to expect favourable outcomes and results. Pessimists, by contrast, interpret many situations negatively, and expect unfavourable outcomes and results. Optimists concentrate on problem-focused coping – making and enacting specific plans for dealing with sources of stress. In addition, they seek social support – the advice and help of friends and others – and refrain from engaging in other activities until current problems are solved and stress is reduced.

Hardiness: viewing stress as a challenge Hardy people appear to differ from others in three respects. They show a higher level of commitment – deeper involvement in their jobs and other life activities; control – the belief that they can, in fact, influence important events in their lives and the outcomes they experience; and challenge – they perceive change as a challenge and an opportunity to grow rather than as a threat to their security.

Consequences of stress These include a noticeable decline in physical appearance; chronic fatigue and tiredness; frequent infections, especially respiratory infections; health complaints, such as headaches, backaches, stomach and skin problems; signs of depression; change in weight or eating habits.

Emotional symptoms include boredom or apathy; hopelessness; cynicism and resentfulness; depressed appearance, sad expressions, slumped posture; expressions of anxiety, frustration, tearfulness.

Behavioural symptoms include absenteeism; accidents; increase in alcohol or caffeine consumption; increase in smoking; obsessive exercising; being irrational and quick to fly off the handle; reduced productivity: inability to concentrate or complete a task.

the condensed idea
Stress is different things to different people

08 Visual illusions

Artists have always been interested in visual and optical illusions. Some, like Escher, are famous for rejoicing in ambiguous and impossible figures. Whole schools of art, like 'op art', explored the nature of visual and optical illusions both of 'stationary' but also moving art.

There are illusions of brightness and colour as well as shape and form. There are physiological illusions that 'baffle' for physical reasons, but most are cognitive illusions. Many are very well known and named after their discoverers, like the Necker cube or the Poggendorf illusion. There are websites dedicated to showing off some of the most famous illusions, of which there are around 20.

> **For it is a certain maxim, no man sees what things are, that knows not what they ought to be.**
>
> Jonathan Richardson, **1715**

It has been suggested that all illusions fall into one of four groups: ambiguities, distortions, paradoxes and factions. Of course illusions are of particular interest to visual scientists and cognitive psychologists because they give an important insight into the process of perception.

The mechanisms Perception is the process by which we recognize what is represented by the information provided by our sense organs. It is a rapid, automatic, unconscious process. It is not a deliberate process, and our awareness of the process of visual perception usually comes only after it is complete: we get the finished product, not the details of the process.

So how does it work? What actually happens from when information enters our senses and us perceiving what is there? It's hard to understand and one of the most successful ways psychologists have found to explain this process is to study visual illusions to discover what they mean.

timeline

1637
Descartes writes about size constancy

1704
Newton describes the rainbow illusion

Figure and ground What we see is classified as either the object we are looking at (figure) or (back)ground. The classification of an item as a figure or ground is not an intrinsic property of the object but depends on the observer. We can always separate them from each other although sometimes we receive ambiguous clues about what the object is and what is the background. Look at the object in figure 1 – is it a vase or two faces? The figure and the ground can be reversed, revealing two different pictures. Can you see the saxophone player and the woman's face in figure 2? Which one do you see first and why?

Fig. 1

Boundaries One of the most important aspects of form perception is the existence of a boundary. If the visual field contains a sharp and distinct change in brightness, colour or texture, we perceive an edge. Figures 3 and 4 show how we 'see' illusory contours (lines that do not exist). In the middle of both pictures triangles can be seen to be brighter than the rest of the picture. This follows the gestalt principle of *closure*, as we tend to complete incomplete forms and fill in the gaps.

Fig. 2

Gestalt principles Psychologists are naturally interested in all aspects of how we see our world: how we see colour, movement and depth, how we recognize objects and people, and indeed the whole debate on whether subliminal perception occurs. At the most abstract level it is possible to distinguish three processes: the *reception* of the light waves by the cornea and iris; *translation*, where this physical energy (light) is coded into neurochemical messages sent to the brain; and *decoding* or translation of these.

Fig. 3

One central feature of study is how we 'put together' or form complete pictures of objects from the separate pieces of information that we have. Between the First and Second World Wars the gestalt psychologists studied the issue of what is called perceptual organization. These psychologists specified various 'laws' – the laws of proximity and good continuation, which tried to explain how we see patterns in abstract shapes. Collectively they are known as the laws of grouping and remain accurate descriptions of how we see.

Fig. 4

1860
Helmholtz writes about 'the intelligent eye'

1884
Müller–Lyer illusion published

1973
Gregory and Gombrich, *Illusions in Nature And Art*

The perceived length of a line depends on the shape and position of other lines that enclose it.

A. Reber, 1985

Fig. 5   Fig. 6

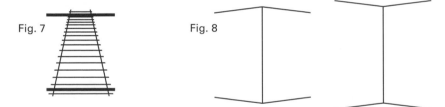

The gestaltists also became particularly interested in the accuracy of what we see. In the late 19th century a group of German psychologists had devised gestalt psychology – a theory of form perception with laws of *pragnanz* (meaning 'good figure') that explain how we perceive. *Similarity* (figure 5) is where similar parts of a form are more likely to be perceived as belonging together. This might depend on relationships of form, colour, size or brightness. The *proximity* (figure 6) principle holds that surfaces or edges close together are more likely to be part of the same object than those far apart. Other principles include continuity, common-fate and symmetry.

Fig. 7   Fig. 8

The Ponzo illusion and Müller–Lyer illusions

It has been argued that these illusions can be explained by assuming that previous knowledge of three-dimensional objects is misapplied to these two-dimensional patterns.

In the Ponzo illusion (figure 7) the two horizontal lines are exactly the same length even though the lower line appears to be much shorter. This is because the linear perspective created by the converging lines of the rail track suggest the top line is further away. If it has the same retinal size but is further away it must be bigger – our perceptual system is mistakenly taking distance into account.

The Müller–Lyer illusion (figure 8) has a similar explanation. The left line looks like the outside corners of a building, while the right line looks like the inside corners. These inside corners are, in a sense, further away than the outside ones, so the right line is perceived as further away and, using the same logic as the Ponzo illusion, as it has the same retinal size it is perceived as longer. These illusions show that perception is influenced by factors other than stimulus – in this case, perceived distance and previous experience.

Constancies When objects move close or far away, under different lights, or turn around, we tend not to see them as different or changing but remaining the same object. There are different types of constancy processes – shape, size, colour, brightness – which can help explain visual illusions.

Pick up this book. Hold it upright and facing you. It is a rectangle. Now flip it over first through a vertical plane, then horizontal. It is no longer the same shape but you see the book as remaining the same. This is shape constancy. Similarly, when we see an elephant walking away from us it does not appear to be getting smaller though the image on the retina quite clearly is.

Culture and the carpentered world Imagine you grew up in an environment where there were no straight lines: no square houses, straight roads, long poles or traditional oblong tables. Your houses were round, as were your fields. Your paths were twisting and turning. Would you still be 'fooled' by visual illusions? If you have never seen a straight road or railway track, would you experience the Ponzo illusion or if you had never seen the corner of a room or house, would you experience the Müller–Lyer illusion?

Various studies have been done with rural African and Aboriginal groups to test ideas about how learning and experience influence our interpretation of illusions. One study compared urban and rural Africans who looked with one eye at a trapezoid shape, called the Ames window, revolving. As predicted, the rural group saw it oscillating around 180 degrees. Another study found Zulus from South Africa saw the Ponzo illusion to a greater extent than white South Africans, possibly due to their greater experience of wide open spaces. So our personal and cultural experiences may make us more or less likely to see visual illusions.

> **The perception of form is entirely a matter of experience.**
> **John Ruskin, 1890**

the condensed idea
Why do our eyes play tricks on us?

09 Psychophysics

Psychophysics (the physics of the mind) is the systematic study of the relationship between the physical characteristics of stimuli and the sensations they produce. This description is functional, or process oriented, because the processes of the sensory systems are of interest, rather than their structure (physiology).

The physics of sensation A simple psychophysics question becomes 'What is the chain of events that begins with a stimulus and leads up to reports such as "a bright red", or "a loud noise"?' The details of this sequence obviously differ for each sense but there are always three basic steps: a stimulus to a sense receptor; a neural chain of events caused by this stimulus – it is changed into an electric signal and then into a nerve impulse; a psychological response to the message (sensation).

Thresholds To study perceptual phenomena, the early psychologists had to find reliable ways to measure people's sensations. One of the central concepts of psychophysics is that of a *threshold*. This is the intensity level of a stimulus required to yield a response. The absolute threshold specifies the least energy required to get a response. So one could specify the softest sound or weakest light that would be required before anyone could detect that sound or light. A difference threshold is the smallest change that is required for a person to detect a change in the stimulus.

> **The magnitude of a sensation is proportional to the logarithm of the intensity of the stimulus causing it.**
> **Fechner's law, 1860**

The just-noticeable difference (jnd) The jnd, or difference threshold, is defined as the smallest difference between two similar stimuli that can be distinguished. This is dependent on both the size and the intensity of that response.

timeline

1834	1860
Weber's law	Fechner's law

Gustav Fechner was the first to use the jnd to measure a person's sensations, in a famous experiment in the 1850s looking at a person's response to brightness. Each subject can see two light disks, the brightness of which is adjustable. The brightness of one is increased until the participant can just detect a difference, the value of which is 1 jnd. The disks are then reset and again one increases until 1 jnd is detected. This is repeated to get the range of a person's sensation for the brightness stimulus.

Fechner was responsible for one of the basic laws of psychophysics: sensation increases as a function of the logarithm of stimulus intensity. This means that the reported strength of a particular sensation increases at a much slower rate than the intensity of the stimulus that causes the sensation. So, for a person to report one light being twice as bright as another, there must be more than twice as much light in the comparison light.

> **Psychophysical law: any formulation of the relation between physical stimulus and sensory process.**
>
> **J. Drever, 1966**

Ernst Heinrich Weber was responsible for another famous psychophysics law. He discovered that the difference threshold is related to the ratio of the intensity of one stimulus to the intensity of another. So, suppose you play a person a sound of 50 decibels, and they can detect a sound of 55 as louder, but not 54: if the sound is 70dB it will have to be 77 for them to detect the difference; if it is 30dB then 33; 100 then 110. In each case the ratio is a constant 1:10. Studies in the 1940s were able to put numbers on this: for brightness it was 1.2 per cent difference, for the taste of salt 20 per cent.

Methods The early psychophysicists and those today still working in the area have come up with various well-tried and trusted methods to study their topic. One is the method of adjustments (or average error). Here people adjust a sound, light or smell so that it is, in their view, identical to one they saw earlier. In the method of limits, a person is asked to judge whether a second stimulus is greater than, less than, or equal in intensity to a previously-seen stimulus. With the method of constant stimuli, people are asked to try to recognize a stimulus in a series of different trials.

1870s	1961	1966
Psychophysics heralds the onset of scientific research	Stevens' law	Signal detection theory developed

> **The eye – it cannot choose but see**
> **We cannot bid the ear be still**
> **Our bodies feel; where'er they be**
> **Against or with our will.**
> **W. Wordsworth, 1847**

Scaling Measurement is all-important in the precise world of psychophysics and it is therefore crucial to have good scales to measure the phenomena. There are four basic properties of all scales: first they show difference (male vs female, hot vs cold); second, magnitude (Great Danes are bigger than Jack Russells); third, equal intervals (the difference between scales is identical, so the difference between 5 and 8 kilograms is the same as that between 22 and 25 kilograms). The final property is that there is a true zero point, indicating the point at which the thing measured does not exist.

Psychologists distinguish between four types of scales: *nominal* (showing difference), *ordinal* (showing difference and magnitude), *interval* (showing difference, magnitude and equal intervals), and *ratio* (with all three components). So exam marks are ordinal, though they may appear interval, while we measure temperature, weight and sight on ratio scales.

Signal detection theory Signal detection theory (SDT) is used when psychologists want to measure the way we make decisions under conditions of uncertainty. People have to decide whether or not they have detected a stimulus, which depends on both their sense organs and their expectancy about the stimulus as well as their motivation to be accurate.

		Event	
		signal	noise
Respond	'yes'	hit	false alarm
	'no'	miss	correct rejection

SDT is used extensively in research today and is perhaps the greatest legacy of the later days of psychophysics. A threshold is not a fixed value, as two human factors play a major role in their detection. One is *sensitivity*: how well the subject can see/hear the stimulus. The other is *response bias*: how readily they say 'yes' to a stimulus when unsure. SDT assumes that the decision maker is not a passive receiver of information, but one who actively makes difficult perceptual judgements under conditions of uncertainty, making signal detection more systematic.

To do this, experimenters put in 'catch trials' where during the experiment no change in stimulus occurs (noise) and the response is checked (see table). Signal detection terminology has *hits* as saying 'yes' to a stimulus, *misses* are saying 'no' to a stimulus; *false alarm* is responding 'yes' to no change, and *correct rejection* is a correct 'no'. If a person wants to be sure to find all stimulus changes, they will risk more false alarms to ensure more hits. Alternatively, people fear false alarms to the point of making misses. A person's response bias can have obvious repercussions for an investigator's estimate of the threshold of detection. To correct for this, psychologists deliberately manipulate a person's response bias and observe the results of these manipulations on a subject's decisions. These effects are expressed graphically on a receiver operating characteristic curve.

An SDT study on acupuncture

One central question in acupuncture is whether the needles reduce pain or patients are simply responding to suggestions. Critics wonder whether reports are of the real analgesic action of the needles or the raising of the patient's subjective thresholds for pain itself. That is, they feel better because their threshold for pain has been increased in the treatment. One early study looked at this pain threshold hypothesis. People were given a hot stimulus on the forearm and asked to rate its intensity from 1 – 12 (nothing – intolerable). Ratings were made before, during and after acupuncture. The treatment did reduce the pain but the data showed that the patients raised their threshold as a result of the acupuncture.

SDT is the best way to determine a person's sensitivity to the occurrence of a perceptual change. A person decides whether a stimulus occurs and therefore other factors are involved including motivation and prior experience.

the condensed idea
Subjective sensations and perceptions can be measured

10 Hallucinations

**'Are thou not, fatal vision, sensible to feeling as to sight?
Or art thou a dagger of the mind, a false creation, proceeding
from the heat-oppressed brain?'** Shakespeare: *Macbeth* 1606

Definition The origin of the word 'hallucination' contains two features: 'to dream' and 'to be distraught'. It is supposedly derived from the Latin *alucinari*, meaning 'to wander in mind'. Ordinary people may speak of their imagination 'playing tricks with them' rather than hallucinations when they are very preoccupied or interested in what is going on around them.

A hallucination is, quite simply, the perception of something – a noise, smell, sight – that is not there. A hallucination involves sensing something while awake and conscious that is not actually physically present. It is sensation without stimulus. A sensory hallucination may include hearing voices of long-dead or mythical people, or it may be of insects crawling on or under the skin. It may be of angels or fairies dancing in bright lights. Some hallucinations are highly idiosyncratic, many transient, unreal and bewildering.

It is important to make various distinctions between hallucinations, illusions and delusions. An illusion is a real reaction to a real sensation with a misattributed cause. Hence the fascination with artistic, or visual, illusions or, indeed, with 'illusion artists' who appear to do impossible things like saw people in half. A delusion is about real reaction to a real sensation but which is given an unreal, impossible, bizarre or overly significant cause.

Different types Hallucinations are known to be associated with many things, including sleep (particularly sleep deprivation), certain drug use (the obviously termed hallucinogens), mental illness (particularly psychosis) and very specific neurological illnesses. Hallucinations occur

timeline

1950s	1960s
Penfield's electrical brain stimulation causes hallucinations	LSD experimenters report rich hallucinations

often in schizophrenic episodes and are described in psychiatric manuals as 'a running commentary on the person and two or more voices conversing with each other'.

Some are mild and common like *hypnagogic* hallucinations, which occur while falling asleep, or the opposite (*hypnopompic*), which occur while waking. Often through the use of very specific drugs people can have the oddest hallucinations. *Chromatopsia* is seeing everybody and everything as the same colour. Those suffering from *Lilliputian* hallucinations see imaginary people in miniature and often with pleasant accompanying feelings. On the other hand, those experiencing *Brodnignagian* hallucinations see everybody as giants.

There are also interesting and unusual cases of pseudo-hallucinations. These occur when the person vividly experiences a hallucination but knows it to be such: that is, they recognize that it has no external foundations. Hallucinatory episodes may follow a particular course. First, something like a particular memory or a sound sparks off the hallucination. The person then tests if it's real and begins to believe it is. The fantasy, distortion and unreality continue to grow and get confused with actual perception.

Auditory hallucinations 'Hearing voices' is perhaps one of the most well known 'signs of madness'. It is particularly associated with the psychotic disorders such as schizophrenia. People hear voices of specific or unidentifiable people when others present cannot hear them. Some who experience these hallucinations appear to be straining to listen for these voices; others talk to themselves, sometimes pausing as if they are in conversation. Occasionally they shout at people not physically present.

Hearing voices occurs less when a person is in conversation with a real person present. People hear voices mostly when they are alone. Other forms of auditory hallucination may involve hearing music – often very familiar music that has powerful emotional associations. This can occur if listening to very loud music for very long periods of time.

> **Hallucination. A perceptual experience with all the compelling subjective properties of a real sensory impression but without the normal physical stimulus for that sensory mobility.**
>
> A. Reber, 1985

1980s	1980s	2000s
Hallucinosis described	Better antipsychotic drugs developed	Distinction between hallucination-induced and related disorders

Causes

There are many different causes for experiencing persistent, often distressing hallucinations. Indeed it is possible to 'induce' hallucinations in people. When people are sensorily deprived in deserts, or jailed in bare cells for 'brainwashing', they often hear and see hallucinations. Equally, people deprived of sleep or doing very long monotonous tasks may have hallucinations.

The first cause is drugs, including alcohol, marijuana, cocaine, crack, heroin or LSD. The second is high fever, especially in young or old people. Third, they may occur in those with very specific sensory problems like blindness or deafness. People who go deaf often say they hear voices. Similarly, those who have limbs amputated experience phantom limbs with all the movement, even pain, experienced.

Next, hallucinations occur in people with severe physical illnesses like brain cancer, kidney or liver failure. Fifth, they can and do occur if suffering from alcohol-related *delirium tremens* or later-life dementia. Sixth, they are often closely associated with specific, severe, psychotic disorders like post-traumatic stress disorder and schizophrenia. Those who have post-traumatic stress disorder often experience flashbacks. Thus when they hear certain sounds or detect certain smells they are instantly transformed back to times of trauma (like war or accidents) and have powerful flashback hallucinations of particular events. Also in times of great stress and mourning some people hear reassuring voices that calm the senses.

For 50 years brain scientists have known that stimulating specific parts of the brain may lead to hallucinations such as feelings of numbness, tingling, heat or cold or running water. Patients with brain damage or degenerative tissues may experience olfactory hallucinations (nearly always unpleasant) or aural gustatory (taste) hallucinations, which may be pleasant or unpleasant. Similarly, certain neurological problems from the relatively common epilepsy to the rare, like Ménière's disease, have often been associated with very specific, often bizarre hallucinations.

Visual hallucinations People have been reported as seeing animals, innate objects and people not present. They may be 'ghosts' or 'angels' and some involve quite complicated scenes or bizarre situations. Some visual hallucinations are silent but in some, people speak, often directly to the individual experiencing the hallucination and give them specific commands. There are a whole range of highly specific visual illusions with appropriate diagnostic labels. Thus *dysmegalopsia* is seeing objects misshapen or with odd/unusual forms; *micropsia* and *macropsia* are seeing objects as either much smaller or bigger than they really are. *Allesthesia* is perception that changes the place where objects actually are, while *palinopsia* is the sensation that an object that should be visually present has been removed from sight.

Diagnosis and management Diagnosticians go through a structured and systematic medical history interview to try to determine the primary cause of hallucinations. They would first enquire about the very specific nature of the hallucinations – what were they like, when they first occurred, when they typically occur, how long they have been present. Next they ask questions about alcohol, drugs and other medication. They enquire about traumatic and emotional events as well as evidence of physical concomitants of agitation, confusion, fever, headaches and vomiting.

The clinical management starts with attempting to specify possible medical or neurological causes or reactions to particular drugs 'within the context of culturally validated phenomena' (e.g. religious festival, music concerts, etc.). Any serious psychiatric diagnosis should only occur after a very close inspection of the nature of the hallucination and the 'symptoms' that might flow from them.

Explanations There are a number of psychological explanations for the occurrence of hallucinations. Freudians saw hallucinations as projections of unconscious wishes or wants. The idea was that the person experiences as 'real' something they felt but could not express because it was below consciousness.

Cognitive psychologists point to problems in cognition processing, particularly metacognition, which is concerned with the understanding of others' interpretation of events. That is, hallucinations are misinterpretations of others' behaviour.

However, it is the biological psychologists who focus most clearly on the causes. They see hallucinations primarily as deficits in brain states resulting from damage or chemical imbalances. They have been able to locate brain regions and identify pharmaceutical processes that lead to hallucinations.

Nevertheless, explaining why a particular individual has a very particular hallucination remains something of a mystery.

the condensed idea
There are many types and causes of hallucinations

11 Delusions

'The person on the talent show is clearly deluded about their singing ability.'

'That politician appears to have delusions of grandeur.'

'As to her hopes to ever get promoted, I fear she is deluded.'

What are they? A delusion is a fixed, immutable, persistent, false belief with no basis in reality. It is a belief held by an individual or a group that is demonstrably false, completely fanciful or more likely simply self-deceptive. A person with delusions often manifests complete certainty and absolute conviction about their beliefs. They are quite incorrigible, resisting incontrovertible arguments and evidence that they are, quite simply, wrong.

Some religious delusions are impossible to verify and hence falsify. Equally, some delusions have an element of self-fulfilment; for example, where a jealous person accuses an innocent partner who then leaves them for another. In that sense they cause their delusions to come true.

All sorts People have delusions about smell (olfactory), about taste (gustatory), about temperature (thermoceptive) and about touch (tactile). They may experience highly disgusting or very pleasant or very unusual smells when meeting a particular person. They may find ordinary foods (oranges, chocolate, milk) have quite different tastes to what they or others regularly experience. They may find cool objects burning hot, or warm objects as frozen. They may find traditionally smooth objects (like a balloon or cat fur) suddenly very rough or uneven.

The most written about of all delusions, namely paranoia, has been shown to follow various stages: general suspiciousness; selective perception of others; hostility; paranoid 'illumination' where all things fall into place; and finally paradoxical delusions of influence and persecution.

timeline

300BC	1880
Ancient Greeks wrote about paranoid delusions	Kraepelin describes paranoid schizophrenia

Delusions often totally preoccupy people and cause them considerable distress. It should be noted that delusions are different from illusions. We have visual and auditory illusions, for instance, that the Sun goes round the Earth or that ventriloquists' dummies actually speak.

Psychiatry and delusional disorder Psychiatrists may diagnose someone as having a delusional disorder under a number of specific situations. Firstly, a person must manifest one or more non-bizarre delusions for at least a month. Secondly, the person has not met other behavioural criteria for being classified as a person with schizophrenia. Thirdly, auditory and visual hallucinations are not prominent, though tactile and olfactory hallucinations may be. Fourthly, despite the delusions or their behavioural consequences, a person's psycho-social functioning is not essentially impaired so that they are not thought of as particularly odd or bizarre. Fifthly, if the specific delusions have an impact on a person's mood, these mood changes do not last very long. Sixthly, the disturbance is not the result of physiological or medical conditions (like the medication a person is on).

> **'Hence vain deluding joys, the brood of folly, without father bred.'**
> John Milton, **1631**

Sometimes psychiatrists say it is difficult to distinguish from other disorders like hypochondriasis (particularly among those with little self-awareness); body dysmorphic disorder (preoccupation with imagined bodily defects); obsessive-compulsive disorder; or paranoid personality disorder.

The delusions of people with schizophrenia are often clearly bizarre. Thus one might believe their brain has been replaced by that of another person or that one has shrunk to 3 feet tall. On the other hand, non-bizarre delusions are also possible. For instance, people may feel they are being followed, photographed or recorded; that somebody is slowly poisoning them; that their partner is always cheating on them; or that their boss or neighbour is in love with them.

Cause In essence the causes are not known. Current interests in neuropsychology have led some to speculate there are biological features that when malfunctioning may cause or exacerbate the problem. Some have implicated brain structures such as basal ganglia, others the limbic

1911	**1942**	**1980s**
Freud argues persecutory delusions are due to repression and projection	*Folie à deux* described as delusory disorder	Paranoia reclassified as delusory disorder

Types of delusion

Psychiatrists have noticed five clear types of delusions.

Erotomanic They believe another person is seriously in love with them – more in the Hollywood romantic, even spiritual way than in the sexual sense. It is often a famous person (film star, sporting hero) but also powerful superiors at work. While many with this delusion keep it a secret and do very little, others may expend a great deal of energy trying to contact their delusional lover via emails, visits and even stalking them. Most are women but men with the delusions tend to act more boldly and get in trouble with the law, particularly if they believe their 'lover' is in trouble or imminent danger.

Grandiose These are sometimes called delusions of grandeur and are manifest when a person believes (with no evidence) that they are special – they have amazing abilities or perspicacity or have made a vitally important discovery. Often the delusions are religious and those with the disorder believe they have a unique and privileged relationship with 'the Almighty'. Sometimes they feel they are a prominent person and have special relationships with other prominent people.

Jealous This is clearly manifest in the strong, but quite unfounded belief that a partner is unfaithful and cheating on them. Odd bits of 'evidence' are put forward for these claims. They may hire a private detective, attempt to imprison their partner as well as physically and verbally attack them.

Persecutory This is the belief that someone or some group is conspiring against them. They believe they are being cheated, spied on, harassed, gossiped about, poisoned or drugged. They are often angry and resentful, with deep feelings of injustice. Many attempt to quell the persecution by legal means or by appealing to authorities. It is the most common type of all the delusionary disorders. Some even get violent and aggressive towards those they believe are targeting them.

Somatic This is the delusion that one's own body is somehow strange or not functioning properly. It may be the belief that one smells odd or that particular parts (nose, breasts, feet) are particularly odd, misshapen or ugly. Often people with these delusions believe they may have some internal bug, insect or parasite that is destroying or affecting some specific part of their body.

❝Take care your worship, those things over there are not giants, but windmills.❞

Miguel de Cervantes, 1605

system and still others the neocortex. For others, genetic explanations are best because of the fact that so many with delusional disorders have first-degree relatives with this and related disorders.

However, other researchers point to the fact that many with the disorder have had 'difficult' childhoods characterized by instability and turbulence, callousness and coldness. Thus some psychoanalytically inclined psychologists have seen delusions as an impairment in the *ego* defence system aimed to protect and bolster the self. So they see the paranoid or persecutory delusions as an attempt to project onto others things that the individuals do not like to admit in themselves. Treatment includes counselling and psychotherapy but also the use of antipsychotic drugs.

Dissimulation and delusions

Many people claim, quite rightly, that in interviews and on questionnaires people lie, fake or don't tell the truth. Psychologists call this 'dissimulation', but have recently distinguished between two very different types. The first is called *impression management*. This is all about presenting oneself in a positive light, perhaps conveniently forgetting certain things and telling small 'white lies' about others. The second is called *self-deception*. Strictly speaking this is not lying but is more like a delusion. If someone says they have a sense of humour but everyone who knows them says they do not, they are deceiving themselves. Similarly, if someone feels ugly or plain while everyone else believes they are not, this implies a negative self-deception. At interviews some forms of self-deception begin to get close to delusions, though delusions are more difficult to change. Certainly in the face of consistent feedback, it is more likely that a person's self-deceptive tendencies are 'cured' or at least reduced.

the condensed idea
Delusions are many and varied

12 Are you conscious?

We are, most of the time, aware of ourselves, our bodies, our sensations and our thinking. To be conscious means perceiving or noticing with a degree of controlled thought or observation. It means being aware, awake, aroused.

Any creature may be thought of as conscious if they appear capable of responding to the world around them: they are awake and alert; they are self-conscious and self-aware. Some commentators have distinguished between *access consciousness*, which is thinking about thinking or perceiving perceptions; and *phenomenal consciousness*, which is having ideas or imaginings of the quality of things. Events that occur in the mind or brain that we cannot access are called subconscious events. But consciousness does not depend on language, nor is it just self-awareness. We can lose self-awareness when deeply involved in music, for example, but that is different from being physically knocked out.

> **Consciousness . . . is the phenomenon whereby the universe's very existence is made known.**
> **Roger Penrose, 1989**

We probably find it much easier to define when people are unconscious through sleep, drugs or illness. We talk of people who have 'passed out' or are 'not with it'. A puzzle for many brain scientists interested in locating the 'seat of consciousness' is that people can experience massive brain damage without losing general consciousness. Brain damage can certainly lead to specific losses of some contents of consciousness but not consciousness itself. It has been argued that to investigate the neuropsychology of consciousness is easy compared with trying to understand why we have the experience in the first place.

timeline

500BC	1688
Cicero first uses the term	Locke introduces the modern meaning

The experience of being conscious

Conscious experience has various different properties. It is private; it is about experiencing things from many different senses (touch, taste, sound, sight); it is about the products or outcomes of thinking rather than how we think; and it is constantly in a state of flux or change. We talk about 'stream of consciousness'. We can be conscious of having some experience and conscious that we have seen it before.

Psychologists are particularly interested in brain-damaged people who are clearly conscious of all the phenomena around them but are unable to access memories of encountering the same or similar experiences before. Many psychologists believe consciousness arises from brain activity. Some propose a physical account because brain damage and brain chemistry affect consciousness.

> **❝Consciousness, then, is our mode of analysis of the outside world into objects and actions.❞**
>
> **J. Bronowski,** 1970

Historical speculations

Whereas the ancient Greeks wrote a great deal about many psychological topics, consciousness was not one of them. It was René Descartes (1640) ('I think, therefore, I am') and John Locke (1690) who believed consciousness was essential to thought and to personal identity. For a long period the two etymologically similar words 'conscious' and 'conscience' were linked. The meanings were not separated until the 17th century, when 'conscious' referred to ideas of personal identity and 'conscience' to issues of moral judgement.

Around the founding of scientific psychology in Germany psychologists used 'mind' and 'consciousness' interchangeably and used introspective methods to investigate it. Behaviourism tried to abolish consciousness as an issue worthy of scientific research. Even cognitive psychologists interested in things like language comprehension and memory took little interest in the topic. But over the last 20 years it has begun to emerge once again as a serious topic.

The new science

The new science of consciousness is trying to explain how subjective experience arises from neural activity. Researchers may be able to deduce by looking at blood flow patterns in the brain what someone is thinking about. Further, by electrical or drug stimulation of particular areas, as well as surgery, they can bring about smells, sights and

1960s onwards	**1991**	**1994**
Cognitive neuroscience approach to the topic	Dennett, *Consciousness Explained*	Pinker, *The Language Instinct*

sounds quite indistinguishable from reality. These scientists are trying to understand how data from the senses get processed; why some kinds of information are accessible and others hidden. Some scientists believe that identifying the exact neural correlates of consciousness is quite possible, even comparatively easy. What they do find more difficult is to relate brain activity to personal inner experience.

Functions Inevitably psychologists take differing standpoints on the function of consciousness. Aristotelians argued that consciousness is effectively a brain state. Radical behaviourists thought it had little purpose and was epiphenomenal (not of primary importance) and preferred to ignore it.

Psychologists think of it mainly in terms of information processing. We attend to, and process, information. We are very efficient at detecting and processing all sorts of information in our environment. Being aware of how we do this, particularly with new, difficult or complex information is, in effect, consciousness. We also may be aware or assume that other people have very different conscious experiences of the same event from our own. One problem with the functionalist school is that one could argue by their definitions that machines have consciousness.

Evolutionary psychologists are functionalists. They see the development of the cortex as a survival function that helps planning, as well as language and social development. One intriguing behavioural criterion of consciousness is self-recognition: the ability to recognize oneself in the mirror. So consciousness evolved as a response to selective pressure in an intelligent social animal. Consciousness functions to represent, store and clarify perceptions: to make sense of new and ambiguous situations and to make better decisions. Consciousness is a survival kit for higher-order species that allows for thoughtful and planned decisions and reactions.

Conscious unconsciousness: the case of hypnosis

To what extent are hypnotized people aware and consciousness? Fully hypnotized people clearly enter a 'different state': one of deep relaxation and open suggestibility. We know some people are relatively highly prone and others highly resistant to hypnosis. Hypnotized people are suggestible and persuadable. The effect is most dramatically seen when the hypnotist attempts to induce post-hypnotic amnesia (not remembering anything about the hypnosis) alongside post-hypnotic suggestibility, where after the event they follow odd, but specific, instructions given under hypnosis.

Brain scanning has certainly advanced our understanding of this phenomenon, discussed by some as a form of little more than cheap show business. Recent studies suggest that hypnosis is indeed an altered state of consciousness because areas of the brain we know to affect consciousness are all clearly affected by the hypnotic process. In hypnotic amnesia a person can be instructed to forget something, often very important, which can be recalled only under very specific conditions. Hypnotic analgesia has attracted the attention particularly of doctors and dentists because its aim is to reduce pain.

However, some observers have offered fairly mundane explanations for the apparent success of hypnotism. For instance, the idea of getting people to experience pain as a feeling of warmth or numbness may be thought of as a very efficient coping strategy. Alternatively, they may more simply be encouraged to pay less attention to some experiences and more to others. Neo-dissociation theory suggests we give up central control of our thoughts to the hypnotist. Non-state theory states hypnosis is little more than acting, imagination and role enactment and is not an altered state of consciousness. Hypnotized, suggestible people are simply doing what is expected of them, which is pleasing the hypnotist, rather than falling into a special trance-like state.

The Freudian unconscious

Psychologists have long been interested, not so much in consciousness, but its opposite. Some have differentiated between the pre-conscious and the unconscious.
Pre-conscious ideas, desires and wishes can without too much difficulty be brought into consciousness. Indeed the aim of therapy is to bring things from the dark, unknowable unconscious into the pre-conscious and thence the conscious. Self-awareness is in fact a major part of the cure: that is, being aware or conscious of why one behaves in a particular way. Through dream analysis, slips of the tongue and free association, analysts believe they can help patients get a glimpse of the unconscious.

the condensed idea
Consciousness is being aware, awake and aroused

13 Positive psychology

Can you teach people to become happy? Does money bring happiness? Why are some people continuously and outwardly more happy than others? These common and fundamental problems to the human condition were routinely ignored by psychologists until comparatively recently.

Positive psychology Positive psychology is the study of factors and processes that lead to positive emotions, virtuous behaviours and optimal performance in individuals and groups. Although a few, mainly 'self psychologists' were always interested in health, adjustment and peak performance, the study of happiness was thought to be unimportant, even trivial. This probably still remains true: for every 100 serious psychology books and papers there exist 99 on depression; there is only one on happiness. But we have known for 50 years that happiness is not the opposite of unhappiness: they are quite unrelated to each other.

> **Happiness is a mystery like religion and should never be rationalised.**
> **G.K. Chesterton, 1920**

The first books on the psychology of happiness started appearing in the 1980s. Then a few specialist academic journals appeared. But it was not until the turn of the millennium that the positive psychology movement was galvanized into action by significant grant money. Positive psychology has become the research focus of many famous psychologists; today it encompasses considerably more than the study of happiness.

Fundamental concerns The psychology of happiness attempts to answer some very fundamental questions pursued over the years by philosophers, theologians and politicians. The first series of questions is

timeline

1969	1987
Bradburn, *The Structure of Psychological Well Being*	Argyle, *The Psychology of Happiness*

really about definition and measurement of happiness; the second is about why certain groups are as happy or unhappy as they are; and the third concerns what one has to do (or not do) to increase happiness.

Science starts with definitions. So what is happiness? Sometimes it is described as a state of well-being, contentment, peace of mind or fulfilment; something to do with life satisfaction or equally the absence of psychological distress. It has also been described in terms of pleasure, enjoyment and fun. To be in a state of flow is to be happy.

The term most often used by researchers is 'subjective well-being'. It means how individuals make a general overall and personal judgement about their own lives and general satisfaction. That is, it is the individual – not coaches, counsellors or confessors, nor teachers, therapists or theoreticians – who makes the judgement about their own well-being.

A man is happy so long as he chooses to be happy.
A. Solzhenitsyn, 1968

These self-evaluations can be broken down into two component parts: satisfaction at work and home; satisfaction with self vs others. Thus one can be high on one and low on other but they tend to correlate highly. People tend to be relatively stable in their evaluations across all aspects of their lives. They can, and do, fluctuate according to particular circumstances, such as having good fortune (winning the lottery) or getting involved in terrible accidents (becoming paralysed) but tend to return to the level characteristics of the individual after a relatively short period of time.

Measuring happiness Most measurements of happiness are by standardized questionnaires or interview schedules. It could be done by informed observers: those people who know the individual well and see them regularly. There is also experience sampling, when people have to report how happy they are many times a day, week or month when a beeper goes off, and these ratings are aggregated. Yet another form of measurement is to investigate a person's memory and check whether they feel predominantly happy or unhappy about their past. Finally, there are some as yet crude but ever-developing physical measures looking at everything from brain scanning to saliva cortisol levels. It is not very difficult to measure happiness reliably and validly.

1998
Official founding date of *Positive Psychology*

1999
Buckingham and Clifton, *First Break all the Rules*

2002
Seligman, *Authentic Happiness*

Does happiness matter? Indeed it does! The research evidence suggests happy people have strong immune systems so they are healthier and live longer than unhappy people. They tend to be more successful at work and have better personal relationships. They are more attractive to others. They seem to like themselves more than unhappy people and to cope better with all sorts of setbacks. Happy people make better decisions and tend to be more creative. Unhappy people seem to waste time and effort being vigilant for signs of danger or failure. This saps their energy.

There is evidence of heritability of subjective well-being. Twin studies have shown that just as people inherit a propensity or predisposition for depression, so they do for happiness. But environmental factors inevitably play a part, particularly early family home environments. We also know that although people can experience events that cause extreme happiness or unhappiness, they tend to return to the starting point relatively quickly.

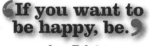

If you want to be happy, be.

Leo Tolstoy, 1900

There is evidence that some societies and individuals are simply happier than others. Thus Latin nations seem happier than Pacific Rim nations. Two things seem to relate to overall national happiness: the wealth, stability and democratic nature of the society in which people live; the social norms and conventions governing the desirability of experiencing positive and avoiding negative emotions. The evidence shows that dire poverty certainly makes people unhappy but great wealth has little effect on subjective well-being. Studies also show that the more materialistic one is, the less happy. The happiest people all seem to have good friends.

Learning to be happy There are many simple things people can do to increase their happiness. The first is not to confuse success with happiness. The next is to take control over their lives and schedules. It has been found that if you act happy (smile, express optimism, be outgoing) it makes others react to you differently and you actually feel happy. Finding work and leisure activities that really engage your skills and passions help a great deal. Having regular exercise, sleeping and eating well help keep up a good mood. Investing time and care in relationships is a very important feature of happiness. Affirming others, helping others and regularly expressing gratitude for life increases happiness, as does having a sense of purpose and hope that may be best described as a faith.

Positive psychology shifts the focus from exploring and attempting to correct or change personal weakness to a study of strengths and virtues. Its aim is to promote authentic happiness and the good life and thereby promote health. A starting point for positive psychology for both popular writers and researchers has been to try to list and categorize strengths and values. This has been done, though it still excites controversy. The following is the current list.

- *Wisdom and knowledge* – creativity, curiosity, open-mindedness, love of learning, perspective.
- *Courage* – bravery, persistence, integrity, vitality.
- *Humanity* – love, kindness, social intelligence.
- *Justice* – citizenship, fairness, leadership.
- *Temperance* – forgiveness and mercy, humility and modesty, prudence, self-regulation.
- *Transcendence* – appreciation of beauty and excellence, gratitude, hope, humour, spirituality.

Positive psychology has now attracted the interest of economists and even theologians and business people. It is a movement that is rapidly gathering momentum and converts to examine scientifically this most essential of all human conditions.

Happiness myths

Researchers have listed a number of myths about the nature and cause of happiness. These include the following, which are widely believed but wrong.

- Happiness depends mainly on the quality and quantity of things that happen to you.
- People are less happy than they used to be.
- People with a serious physical disability are always less happy.
- Young people in the prime of life are much happier than older people.
- People who experience great happiness also experience great unhappiness.
- More intelligent people are generally happier than less intelligent people.
- Children add significantly to the happiness of married couples.
- Acquiring lots of money makes people much happier in the long run.
- Overall, men are happier than women.
- Pursuing happiness paradoxically ensures you lose it.

the condensed idea
We can learn to be happy

14 Emotional intelligence

'Emotional intelligence is an organising framework for categorising abilities relating to understanding, managing and using feelings.' P. Salovey and J. Mayer, 1994

The term 'emotional intelligence' (EI) can be traced back over 40 years, but especially to one influential paper in 1990 and Daniel Goleman's popular book, *Emotional Intelligence* in 1995. It has spawned a huge industry, particularly with those interested in success at work. Many books make dramatic claims; for instance, that cognitive ability or traditional academic intelligence contributes only about 20 per cent to general life success (academic, personal and work) while the remaining 80 per cent is directly attributable to EI.

The components of EI There is no agreement about what features, factors, abilities or skills form part of EI. As more and more tests of, and books about, EI appear on the market, the situation gets worse rather than better. Most, but not all, theories and systems include ideas about emotional awareness and regulation.

A central unresolved question is what are the facets or components of EI? Thus early models distinguished between the perception, appraisal and expression of emotion in self and others; the use of emotion to facilitate thinking; the use of emotional knowledge to understand and analyse emotions; reflective regulation of emotions to promote growth. Some writers talk of *emotional literacy* (the knowledge and understanding of one's own emotions and how they function), *emotional fitness* (trustworthiness and emotional hardiness and flexibility), *emotional depth* (emotional growth and intensity), and *emotional alchemy* (using emotions to discover creative opportunities).

timeline

1920		**1990**
Concept of 'social intelligence' introduced		First published scientific paper on the topic

Others divide up EI into factors like self-awareness, self-regulation, self-motivation, empathy and social skills. One more popular conception has 15 components.

Common facets in salient models of Emotional Intelligence

Facets	High scorers perceive themselves as being or having . . .
Adaptability	Flexible and willing to adapt to new conditions
Assertiveness	Forthright, frank and willing to stand up for their rights
Emotion expression	Capable of communicating their feelings to others
Emotion management (others)	Capable of influencing other people's feelings
Emotion perception (self and others)	Clear about their own and other people's feelings
Emotion regulation	Capable of controlling their emotions
Impulsiveness (low)	Reflective and less likely to give into their urges
Relationship skills	Capable of having fulfilling personal relationships
Self-esteem	Successful and self-confident
Self-motivation	Driven and unlikely to give up in the face of adversity
Social competence	Accomplished networkers with excellent social skills
Stress management	Capable of withstanding pressure and regulating stress
Trait empathy	Capable of taking someone else's perspective
Trait happiness	Cheerful and satisfied with their lives
Trait optimism	Confident and likely to 'look on the bright side' of life

These facets can be combined into four different related but independent factors labelled well-being, self-control skills, emotional skills and social skills.

Measurement EI is often measured as an emotional intelligence quotient (EQ). Psychometricians make a distinction between measures of maximum performance (e.g. IQ tests – right or wrong answers) and measures of typical response (e.g. personality questionnaires – preference answers) with far-reaching implications. Self-report measurement leads to the idea of EI essentially as a personality trait ('trait EI' or 'emotional self-efficacy'), whereas potential maximum-performance measurement would lead to ideas of EI as a cognitive ability ('ability EI' or 'cognitive-emotional ability').

1995	1997	2003
Goleman, *Emotional Intelligence*	First popular self-report questionnaire developed	First ability measure devised

EQ at work

How is EQ correlated with or essential for business success? Consider some of the explanations for how EQ operates in the workplace and why people with higher EI are supposed to be more successful. First, high-EQ people are better at communicating their ideas, intentions and goals. They are more articulate, assertive and sensitive. Second, EQ is closely associated with teamwork social skills, which are very important at work. Third, business leaders, high in EQ, build supportive climates which increase organizational commitment, which in turn leads to success. Fourth, high-EQ leaders are perceptive and know their own and their team's strengths and weaknesses, which enables them to leverage the former and compensate for the latter. Fifth, EQ is related to effective and efficient coping skills which enable people to deal better with demands, pressure and stress. Sixth, high-EQ leaders can accurately identify what followers feel and need, as well as being more inspiring and supportive. They generate more excitement, enthusiasm and optimism. Seventh, high-EQ managers, unlike their low-EQ companions, are less prone to negative, defensive and destructive coping and decision-making styles.

Many dispute the more fundamental point that EI could ever be actually measured by cognitive ability tests. That is, that EI concepts, like emotional regulation, can never be reliably and validly measured by an objective ability test because of the subjective nature of emotional experience. Some argue that trait EI encompasses behavioural tendencies and self-perceived abilities, as opposed to actual cognitive abilities, and belongs in the realm of personality. In contrast, ability EI, which encompasses actual abilities, belongs primarily in the domain of cognitive ability. There are well over a dozen trait EI tests, which look essentially like personality tests.

On the other hand, there are those who see EI as a 'real' intelligence or ability that needs to be measured as such. The most well-established measure is called the MSCEIT, which measures four factors: perceiving and identifying emotions (the ability to recognize how you and those around you are feeling); using emotions to facilitate thought (the ability to generate emotion, and then reason with this emotion); understanding emotions (the ability to understand complex emotions and emotional 'chains' and how emotions evolve); and managing emotions (the ability to manage emotions in yourself and in others).

The MSCEIT asks test-takers to:

- identify the emotions expressed by a face or in designs
- generate a mood and solve problems with that mood
- define the causes of different emotions

- understand the progression of emotions
- determine how best to include emotion in our thinking in situations that involve ourselves or other people.

There are thus two very different ways of measuring EI. One looks like taking a personality test and indeed sees EI as a type of personality trait. The other is more like an ability test. The former measures are much easier and cheaper to administer than the latter. But the real question is which is the more accurate and reliable. Studies have shown that scores from the two tests are modestly positively correlated. At the very heart of the debate is whether EI is just another personality trait or a real part of intelligence.

> **'Emotional intelligence: long neglected core component of mental ability or faddish and confused idea massively commercialised.'**
> **A. Furnham, 2001**

Emotional labour

Many jobs require physical and mental labour but some require emotional labour. Service staff are required to express emotions they do not necessarily feel. They are required to smile, to be positive, to appear relaxed whatever they actually experience. This is called 'surface acting'. In some jobs you are almost required actually to feel the emotions that you display. This is called 'deep acting'. Some customers can spot the false display of emotion so you have to learn the 'inside-out smile'.

Some service workers whose emotions are managed and controlled by their employers become alienated from their real feelings. The sorts of emotions are showing patience, friendliness and curiosity, while suppressing boredom, frustration and anger. One way to do this is through the use of scripts. Service staff are encouraged to act: to learn their lines; to portray a character. This teaches them the appropriate emotion. Similarly, uniforms can act like stage clothes. They can inform and protect.

All service staff have a 'backstage' in the galley, the kitchen, even the cloakrooms. Here they can be themselves, let off steam, react how they would naturally. Behind the scenes they can mock difficult customers. They can get their own back and enjoy the camaraderie of the oppressed. Rest breaks are times to become the real self; to take off the make-up; to recover a sense of self-worth and to take some time off emotional labour.

the condensed idea
Is EI to do with personality, or cognitive ability?

15 What are emotions for?

Emotions are powerful social signals. 'Emotion' and 'motivation' have the same Latin root meaning 'to move'. Emotions send us quick, powerful, physical messages that allow us to respond to our environment. They also enable us to communicate voluntarily or involuntarily.

Evolution has left us with a set of highly adaptive programs, all designed to solve specific survival problems. We all inherit macro and micro emotional programs that are the result of many encounters in the past. We have had to learn who to trust, how to detect sexual infidelity, how to cope with failure and loss of status, how to react to death. The automatic, involuntary expression of many emotions is a key feature of the successful social life of our social species. We have a rich, decodable repertoire of emotional signals to facilitate social interaction. Emotions galvanize and activate many systems together that deal with the problem.

> **Emotions are mental devices for guaranteeing commitment.**
>
> Mark Ridley, 1996

Fear Many fear being followed, ambushed or attacked at night. This fear sets into process a whole set of circumstances or routines. First, you become highly attentive to particular visual or auditory cues; second, your priorities and goals change: hunger, pain, thirst are suppressed in order to achieve safety. Third, your information-gathering systems get focused into particular issues. Fourth, some simple concepts emerge or change from easy and difficult to dangerous or safe. Fifth, memories of past events like this situation are triggered. Sixth, there may be an attempt to communicate rather unusually, like via a loud shout or cry, or indeed the opposite, finding

timeline

1872	1967
Darwin, *The Expression of Emotions in Man and Animals*	Morris, *The Naked Ape*

oneself paralysed by the fear and quite unable to utter a sound. Seventh, an inference or hypothesis-testing system is evoked, meaning people try to work out what is happening and what will happen next. Eighth, learning systems are activated and then, ninth, physiological systems. This may be for a flight-or-fight response which then leads to a series of behavioural decision rules. Thus the person might make a run or even attack.

Recognizing emotions Though disputed, many researchers have accepted that there are six fundamental and distinguishable emotions. These are:

- happiness
- sadness
- surprise
- anger
- disgust
- fear.

Charles Darwin, who was the first to write a scientific treatise on non-verbal emotional expressions, argued that we can recognize distinctive facial expressions that correspond to the fundamental emotional states. They are *manifest emotions*, part of our evolutionary background and are not learnt. Blind people express facial emotions much the same as sighted people. The face has different highly expressive parts, all of which can signal emotion. The eyes can be wide or narrow, the pupils dilated or not, and the eyebrows raised or lowered. The person may blink excessively or stare. The mouth can be opened or remain shut; it can be turned up or down; the teeth and tongue can be seen or hidden. The skin can be blushed or not, with or without signs of perspiration. The nose can have flared nostrils. The angry face has frowning with raised upper eyelid, dilated nostrils, open lips with lower teeth exposed, widened eyes.

❝Emotions occur precisely when adaptation is hindered for any reason whatever.❞

E. Claparède, **1928**

Facial and other non-verbal expressions act as emotional state readouts. However, two caveats are worth considering. The first is the issue of *control* and whether we can easily and accurately control our physical display of emotions. Being surprised or shocked or attacked leads to immediate and strong reactions by the autonomic nervous system. Some emotions appear more under our control than others. Thus, we can supposedly, relatively

1975	**1990s**	**2003**
Argyle, *Bodily Communication*	The concept of the science of emotion used	Collett, *The Book of Tells*

easily, control our gestures and body movements, though research has shown we often 'leak' emotions by particular gestures and foot movements when stressed. Equally, most of us feel we have less control over our pupil dilation and heart rate.

The second issue concerns (conscious) awareness of emotions. Sometimes both sender and receiver are fully aware, as in the case of them blushing. Equally, neither might be aware of small gaze shifts, eyebrow movements or pupil dilation. Experts are trained to be aware of particular non-verbal correlates of emotional states such as clamped or sealed smiles, yawning and head movements. Finally, emotional message senders may be aware of their message but receivers unaware when they are trying to hide something.

Encoding and decoding emotions People communicate emotionally: people show their emotions through facial expression, voice changes, body movement and posture. Physiological arousal initiates specific reactions that cause characteristic expressions. Thus fear leads to a restricted flow of blood to skin and muscles (and hence the white face) while for anger the opposite (the 'purple rage') occurs.

Man watching

Desmond Morris's book *The Naked Ape*, published in 1967, was an evolutionary account of human behaviour. His argument is that we are animals (a species of primates) and therefore a biological phenomenon dominated by biological rules. His technique was to observe *Homo sapiens* as a zoologist trying to understand the meaning of behaviour or specific actions. The idea is that zoological training in evolutionary theory and close observation can allow us to devise a field guide to human behaviour. This explains many of the everyday actions, gestures and signals we send and receive that have emotionally relevant content.

What caused so much interest in the book was the close description of particular behaviours like eye gaze, self-touching or status display and explaining their meaning and function from an evolutionary perspective.

Infants detect and respond to different emotions in their caregiver from a very early age. They show characteristic reactions to anger, disgust and fear. Later they display characteristic and detectable emotional states: distress (crying, hand in mouth); anger (screaming, temper tantrums); frustration (scratching the body, teeth grinding, kneading the feet).

Just as we have been programmed, but also taught, to encode specific emotions, so we have learnt to decode them. Early studies showed people clearly expressing emotions like joy, fear, surprise and anger.

Some were shown silent films, others films with sounds, while others just heard a sound track. Surprise and contempt were the most difficult emotions to recognize or decode while fear, anger and joy were the easiest.

People use many cues to decode the emotions of others. There are conflicting cues such as someone with a smiling mouth but expressionless eyes. Indeed it is assumed that non-verbal communication is much more powerful than verbal or vocal communication because it is more honest, and more difficult to fake.

Measuring emotions Psychologists tend to use four methods to measure most things in the area. The first is self-report or what people say about themselves. This can be done via interview or questionnaire. The second is observation or what others say about a person they know or whom they are observing. The third method is to measure the person's behaviour while doing a task. The final measurement is physiological, including everything from blood and saliva samples, through heart and breathing monitoring to electrical signals in the brain.

> **Sorrow is tranquillity remembered in emotion.**
> **Dorothy Parker, 1939**

Thus you ask somebody to describe their emotions – how they feel or felt. Or you could ask an observer or group how someone appeared when giving a speech. You could also measure how fast or slowly a person spoke or moved in a particular situation compared to how they are 'normally'. Or you could measure a person's heart rate, breathing or cortisol level soon after or during a particular episode.

Part of the problem is that there is so little concordance between the various measures. Thus a person may say they were very nervous but observers did not detect it. Equally a person may report not being overly anxious during a performance, yet various physiological measures show very high levels of arousal. Another related problem is that there are different physiological markers of the different emotions. Physiological measures can be very crude and it is difficult to describe with any certainty what a person is or was feeling based on physiological data.

the condensed idea
Emotions have an evolutionary purpose

16 Cognitive therapy

'Attribution processes are to be understood, not only as a means of providing the individual with a veridical view of his world, but as a means of encouraging and maintaining his effective exercise of control in that world.' H.H. Kelley, **1972**

Pioneers in the area It is often assumed that cognitive therapy (CT) began in the 1960s. The father figure of this form of psychotherapy is recognized to be Aaron Beck, who wrote *Depression: Causes and Treatment* in 1967 and *Cognitive Therapy and the Emotional Disorders* in 1976. A second founding figure of this approach was Albert Ellis (1914–2007), who developed what is called rational emotive behaviour therapy. He talked of the ABC of irrational beliefs: the activating event, the belief associated with it, and the consequences (emotional and behavioural) of that approach. His technique was called reframing or reinterpreting, which encourages a reinterpretation of events and the development of healthy coping strategies. As a therapy it has proved particularly effective with those who set themselves high standards or who ruminate and feel guilty about their own perceived inadequacies.

Thinking therapy Cognitive therapy was preceded by behaviour therapy and is sometimes called behaviour modification. Thus a phobic person may slowly but deliberately be exposed to the very situations that cause fear in order to provide evidence that these fears have no objective basis. Behaviour modification also uses aversive therapy, which pairs an unpleasant experience with a particular activity – giving an alcoholic a drug that makes them vomit every time they drink; painting nail-biters' nails

timeline

1965	**1967**
Behaviourists admit private thoughts were behaviours	Beck, *Depression: Causes and Treatment*

with very bitter paint, and so on. In institutions token-economies are extensively used where people receive a token (exchangeable for goods or privileges) if they behave in clearly prescribed ways. You encourage good behaviour like smiling or talking by giving a person a token every time they voluntarily manifest the behaviour.

The central concept is that therapists need to investigate how people perceive and interpret their world; how they think about and remember events and more particularly how they attribute cause. Hence the word 'cognitive': the idea of the therapy is to explore and then change cognitions.

Cognitive therapists talk of *schemas*, which are ways or filters through which we see the world. People develop cognitive biases which are selective ways in which they see and interpret events. Thus they may remember their total schooling as highly selective, generalized memories of bullying, failure and unhappiness; or achievement, friendship and fulfilment. People seem arbitrary, selective and often prone to generalization in their memory of the past, as well as their current and future view.

> **❝Cognitive behaviour therapy is a great treatment for people who want to help themselves get better.❞**
> **British Medical Journal, 2000**

Cognitive therapy aims to break, and then change, a pattern of behaviour through changes in thinking. The aim is to replace vicious cycles with virtuous cycles through the interpretation of events. Thus a person may attend a party but fail to talk to people; which makes them think they must be boring or unattractive; which in turn leads them to feel depressed and thus avoid future parties or turn down requests; which leads to fewer invitations. The resulting feeling is of being socially unskilled, inept or ugly. The therapy would start by considering other reasons why few people speak or spoke to them at the particular party in the first place and changes in the so-called 'logic' that follow from it.

Cognitive therapy for depression CT asserts that most depressed people have learnt a highly negative world view or schema through early experiences in childhood and adolescence. This may have occurred for many reasons: parental depression, parental or peer criticism or

1970	1980	2000
Ellis, *Reason and Emotion in Psychotherapy*	Stress inoculation therapy described	CBT the most widely practised therapy

rejection; death or divorce of a parent. They feel a failure, helpless and hopeless and bound to fail at everything they do. In the words of CT, a negative schema (a pessimistic world view) leads to cognitive biases (mistaken beliefs) which sources the negative schema and thence through self-fulfilling prophesies leads to failure.

> **Surveys of therapists indicate that CBT is fast becoming the majority orientation of practicing psychologists.**
>
> Brandon Gaudiano, 2008

Depressed people develop a particular attribution or explanatory style of viewing what happens to themselves and others. This has three components: internal–external (whether the cause is internal to them or external), stable–unstable (whether the cause is temporary, like mood, or more stable, like ability) and global–specific (whether it affects all aspects of one's life or very specific parts).

So the negative or depressive attribution style would explain failure (in an exam; to get promotion; a relationship) as internal ('my fault'), stable (because of my lack of ability; odd personality) and global (will affect all aspects of my life). On the other hand, one could explain a failure to pass a driving test as external (the driving instructor; the weather on the day), unstable (which changes or can be changed) and specific (affecting only the driver's licence).

Cognitive behaviour therapy (CBT) Currently probably the most widely used of all therapies for a very wide range of conditions, CBT grew out of cognitive therapy, rational emotive behaviour therapy and behaviour modification. CBT is based on four assumptions. Firstly, people interpret events rather than see what actually happens to them. Secondly, thoughts, feelings and behaviour are all interlocked, interwoven and interrelated. Thirdly, for therapy to work it must clarify, then change how people think about themselves and others. Fourthly, therapy should aim to change both beliefs and behaviours, because the benefits and effects are greater if both are attacked at the same time.

Typical phases include obtaining a detailed behavioural diary of significant everyday events and all the thoughts, feelings and behaviours associated with them; interrogating all beliefs and behaviours that are maladaptive or unhelpful; after that, trying to approach specific situations with a very different mindset while avoiding others altogether. Other techniques like relaxation may also be taught. Clients are encouraged to self-monitor and be introspective: to look at how they really think about and react to themselves, other people and the world in general.

The focus is always on cognitions and changing biases and distortions into more realistic and positive beliefs. Its target is automatic, irrational thoughts that often lead to depression. It seems to be particularly effective with people suffering from anxiety, depression, obsessive-compulsive disorder and panic attacks.

Efficacy

Supporters of CBT claim it is cost-effective, adaptable and it works. Some reports suggest that it has a 50 per cent 'cure rate' for a short-term 'course', which is thought of as very successful. Thus if a person attends 16 one-to-one sessions once a week there is a 50:50 chance they will lose their psychiatric symptoms and not relapse. In severe cases, when used with appropriate medication it appears to have the best chances of helping a client, particularly with depression.

Cognitive behaviour therapy is more effective than cognitive therapy on its own. Both, however, are only modestly effective with serious psychotic illnesses like schizophrenia. Cognitive therapists tend to underplay physical factors and physiological processes which we are beginning to understand have an important part to play in depression, distress and many mental illnesses. Further, it has been shown that cognitive therapy can really change irrational and distorted thinking in certain clients without having much effect or change on their maladaptive behaviour.

It is difficult to measure the true efficacy of any particular therapy for many reasons. Patients differ in the severity of their condition. Much depends on the personality, ability and skills of the therapist and the 'fit' or chemistry between client and therapist. Short-term effects may wear off, with various relapses, and measurement must be done over long periods of time. Some people drop out of therapy and it is not certain who or why. Further, many patients – often unbeknown to their therapist – are partaking of other therapies like alternative and complementary medicine, yoga, vitamin supplements, self-help. It is therefore not clear which is having which effect.

the condensed idea
Cognitive therapy can change thought and behaviour

17 IQ and you

'An intelligence test sometimes shows a man how smart he would have been not to have taken it.' L. Peter, 1968

The meaning of IQ

Sir Francis Galton was the first clear advocate of intelligence tests. He seems to have believed that intelligence was a single general ability, that it was largely inherited and that it could best be measured in terms of the speed of problem-solving and other related mental processes.

Although experts still cannot agree on an exact definition of intelligence, themes common to many of their definitions are that intelligence is the ability to learn from experience, and the ability to adapt to the environment.

Some people are seen as acute, astute, bright, brilliant, capable, keen, quick-witted and sharp. Others are perceived to be dim, dull, half-witted, slow or stupid. The former tend to be analytical and articulate: they learn fast, they remember things well and they can explain complex issues. The latter are the opposite. Smart people tend to be better at school and at work.

Popular views 'Intelligence is what an intelligence test measures and that is all.' Many lay people are deeply sceptical about the use of intelligence tests. But are they correct?

The intelligent person is believed to solve problems well, reason clearly, think logically, and have a good store of information, but also able to balance information and show intelligence in worldly as well as academic contexts. Ordinary people tend to downplay analytical abilities, stressing instead unconventional ways of thinking and acting. Also, aesthetic taste, imagination, inquisitiveness and intuitiveness are part of lay theories, most of which go way beyond conventional psychological tests of creativity.

timeline

1903
Binet develops a French intelligence test for use in schools

1904
Thorndike, *An Introduction to the Theory of Mental and Social Measurements*

Many studies have shown that males give higher self-estimates than females for intelligence (cognitive ability), particularly spatial and mathematical intelligence, but that for estimates of emotional intelligence it is the other way around. Overall, however, people are not that good at estimating their actual scores, with some people showing humility, that is underestimating their actual ability, with others showing hubris by overestimating the score that they actually achieved.

The history of testing In 1904 the French Ministry of Education asked psychologist Alfred Binet to devise a method to identify children who would have difficulty keeping up in regular classes. Binet produced a test designed to measure a person's ability to reason and use judgement. He created the test items by identifying questions that could be answered by average children of different ages.

The child was first asked questions slightly below his or her age level and then was asked questions of increasing difficulty. Testing stopped when the child failed to answer all the questions at a particular specified age level. Binet's test was scored by noting the age level at which the child answered all the questions correctly, and then adding two months' extra credit for each additional answer at the next level. Thus, a child who correctly answered all the questions to the 9-year-old level test plus three questions above the 9-year-old level was identified as having a 'mental age' of 9 years and 6 months.

Binet's test was introduced to the US by Lewis Terman. Instead of calculating mental age as Binet had done, Terman used a measure called the intelligence quotient (IQ), which meant dividing mental age by chronological age and multiplying by 100. Thus, an 8-year-old child with a mental age of 10 years would have an IQ of 125 (10 divided by 8 equals 1.25; 1.25 multiplied by 100 equals 125). This way of calculating IQ was used until 1960, when it was replaced by a measure called the deviation IQ, calculated by comparing a person's score with the distribution of scores obtained by the general population. This shows where a person stands in relation to other people of that age and group (ethnic, religious, national).

> ‘Some men are born mediocre, some men achieve mediocrity, and some men have mediocrity thrust upon them.’
>
> **Joseph Heller, 1961**

1916	1923	1939
Stanford-Binet test published	Spearman, *The Nature of Intelligence and the Principles of Cognition*	Wechsler Adult Intelligence Scale developed

Thus with IQ, we know that 66 per cent of people score between 85 and 115 and that 97 per cent score between 70 and 130. There are very few gifted (over 130) or retarded (under 70) people. Studies show that most professional people score over 120 while most unskilled workers score between 90 and 110.

A summary of what psychologists think about intelligence
The publication of a highly controversial book on intelligence (*The Bell Curve*, Richard J. Herrnstein and Charles Murray, 1994) and passionate – although not necessarily well-informed – debate, led over 50 of the world's experts to establish what they believe to be an excellent and clear statement on what psychologists think about intelligence.

The meaning and measurement of intelligence
- Intelligence is a general mental capability that involves the ability to reason, plan, solve problems, think abstractly, comprehend complex ideas, learn quickly and learn from experience.
- The spread of people along the IQ continuum, from low to high, can be represented well by the bell curve ('the normal curve').
- Intelligence tests are not culturally biased against any racial groups.
- The brain processes underlying intelligence are poorly understood.

Group differences
- Members of all racial-ethnic national groups can be found at every IQ level.
- The bell curve for whites is centred roughly around IQ 100; the bell curve for American and African blacks roughly around IQ 85.

Practical importance
- IQ is strongly related to many important educational, occupational, economic and social outcomes and is very strong in some areas in life (education, military training), moderate but robust in others (social competence), and modest but consistent in others (law-abidingness).
- Whatever IQ tests measure, it is of great practical and social importance.
- A high IQ is an advantage in life because virtually all activities require reasoning and decision-making. Nothing guarantees failure in life but the odds for success in our society are greater with higher IQs.
- Having a higher IQ is more important, the more complex (novel, ambiguous, changing, unpredictable or multifaceted) the job/task that people do.

- Differences in intelligence certainly are not the only factor affecting education, training and job differences, but intelligence is often the most important.
- Personality traits, talents, aptitudes and physical capabilities are important in many jobs, but less important than intelligence.

Source and stability of within-group differences

- Heritability estimates range from 0.4 to 0.8 (on a scale from 0 to 1); genetics plays a bigger role than does environment in creating IQ differences among individuals.
- Members of the same family differ substantially in intelligence for both genetic and environmental reasons.
- IQ is affected by the environment and people. Individuals are not born with fixed, unchangeable levels of intelligence.
- Experts do not know yet how to manipulate it to raise or lower IQs permanently.
- Genetically caused differences are not necessarily irremediable.

Source and stability of between-group differences

- IQs for different racial-ethnic groups are converging.
- Race differences in IQ are the same when youngsters leave school as when they enter it.
- The reasons that blacks differ among themselves in intelligence is the same as those for why whites differ.
- There is no definite answer to why there are differences across racial-ethnic groups.
- Racial differences are smaller but still substantial for individuals from the same socio-economic backgrounds.
- Because research on intelligence relies on racial self-classification, different findings relate to some unclear mixture of social and biological distinctions among groups (no one claims otherwise).

Implications for social policy

- The research findings neither dictate nor preclude any particular social policy.

> **Intelligence is quickness to apprehend as distinct from ability, which is capacity to act wisely on the thing apprehended.**
>
> **A.N. Whitehead, 1960**

the condensed idea
What is an intelligence quotient?

18 Flynn effect

Are students getting cleverer? It seems to be the case that school and university marks are consistently on the rise in many countries. Year after year the government boasts these results, suggesting they are due to factors like better teaching and investments into more facilities at schools. Some people argue that examinations are simply getting easier. It could also be that students are working harder and being more conscientious. Or could it be that they really are getting more intelligent?

How bright are your relatives? Imagine there was a really good, accurate, fair intelligence test. This test ensured that it gave a clear, specific reading of your actual total intellectual capability and capacity. Like all intelligence tests, this gives a score on a bell curve where 100 is average (see Chapter 17). We know that 66 per cent of people score between 85 and 115 and 97 per cent between 70 and 130. And you are pretty smart if you score, say, 135 as you are in the top 1 per cent of the population.

The term IQ is bound to the myths that intelligence is unitary, fixed and predetermined.

D. Reschly, 1981

Can you remember your own IQ score? Be honest now – no bragging or false humility! Now what about your parents? What would your mother score, or your father? And what of your grandmother or grandfather? And could you estimate the score of your children? Is there a change in the scores over the generations?

Research in this area shows that people believe that every generation seems to gain about 4–6 IQ points. So your parents are/were brighter than your grandparents, and your children are brighter than you. Every 10 to 15 years we see a jump in national IQ.

timeline

1987

Flynn, 'Massive IQ gains in 14 countries'

1990s

Confirmation of Flynn in many samples

The discovery That may be what people believe, but is it true? It was an American political scientist working in New Zealand, James Flynn, who gave his name to this 'effect'. He noticed two things when he inspected famous and respected IQ test manuals. One was that every so often the norms which describe typical scores for different age, sex and race groups had to change. The other was that every few years, scores in the same age group were growing. In short, people were doing better over time. The tests seemed to be getting easier or we were, as a species, getting brighter – or both. This means a good score in 1990 was a brilliant score in 1970 but only an average score in 2005.

The first thing was to check that this effect was true of many countries and many tests. Well over 20 countries' data have now been examined from America, Australia and Austria to Belgium, Brazil and Britain. Furthermore, it was true over different types of test: tests of fluid or problem-solving intelligence as well as knowledge-based vocabulary tests or crystallized intelligence. One rich data source was that kept by armies who measured the IQ of conscripts to see whether they should or could become fighter pilots or submariners, cooks or military police. The data show that the graph of the average IQ of many thousands of young men in the same country appears to move steadily and remorselessly upwards over time.

> **Flynn is quite right that university professors have not been seen "dancing in the streets" at their students' new-found comprehension and creativity.**
>
> **Chris Brand, 1996**

There seemed to be impressive evidence of 'massive IQ gains', as Flynn claimed. But the central question became: why? Are we really becoming more intelligent? This of course led to the more fundamental question of whether these tests are really measuring intelligence or something else related to intelligence. Flynn never questioned the reliability, validity and usefulness of IQ tests in educational and occupational settings.

At first it was suggested there may be two reasons why IQ scores were rising but actual IQ was not:

- over time it was cleverer people who were tested

1999	2005	2007
Flynn, 'Searching for justice' in *American Psychology*	Evidence that IQ rises peaked in the 1990s	Flynn, *What is intelligence?*

- people were just getting better at taking tests because they were more used to test-taking at school: evidence of a practice effect.

Others say the Flynn effect is real. And they point to height as a similar factor that has increased across generations. We are getting taller, so why not brighter? But there is no record in schools or universities, patent offices or Nobel Prize committees of the real evidence of a rise in IQ over this (relatively short) time period.

The Flynn effect is a phenomenon in search of an explanation.

What this research has certainly demonstrated is that tests must regularly and routinely be restandardized. This can prevent many misinterpretations. Thus people get wrongly classified. For example, it was supposed that people became less good at problem-solving as they got older. But that was

Causes

Explanations have been proposed in a number of areas.

Education In most countries, with every generation people are spending longer at school and with better facilities. Schooling is compulsory and people from all backgrounds have become used to learning and being tested. Intelligence is related to learning; so as education is better and more widespread, scores get higher.

Nutrition People are now better nourished, particularly in childhood, which reduces the incidence of 'backwardness' in the population. There are fewer people who had poor nutrition in youth so the bottom end of the distribution is removed – which means the average score goes up.

Social trends We are all now much more used to timed tests and performing against the clock. People are familiar with tests and testing and so do better overall.

Parental involvement The idea is that parents provide richer home environments for their children and express a greater interest in their education than they used to. They have higher expectations and get involved more. The trend to have smaller families where parents invest more in each of their children may also be an important factor.

Social environment The world is more complex and stimulating. Modernization and new technology mean that people have to manipulate abstract concepts more, and this is essentially what intelligence tests measure.

because they were compared with young people today. If they are compared with scores of their own cohort measured 50 years before, it is apparent that these changes are minimal.

The Flynn effect suggests environmental rather than genetic causes of change in intelligence. While it is perfectly conceivable to argue that brighter people seek out more stimulating environments for themselves and their children, which further increases their IQ, it raises the old arguments about nature and nurture. Thus for the Flynn effect to work, environmental effects can work both ways. So a rich environment and sustained effort can cause IQs to increase. Equally, with poor, polluted environments and with people little interested in personal development, the opposite effect occurs.

> **‘Just as average height has increased over generations, people began to wonder if intelligence was rising.’**
>
> **Chris Brand,** 1996

The end of the rise? Other questions have arisen about whether the Flynn effect has begun to taper off: that is, whether there is now a decline in the increase seen. This means the next generation will not score higher than this generation. Indeed, there is growing scepticism as reports emerge from countries where IQ scores are on the decline or from teachers who say there is no evidence whatsoever that children are getting brighter despite their improved exam results. Evidence now appears to be emerging that if indeed the Flynn effect was once really true, the rise has not only stopped but is in reverse. Some argue that there is now good reason to believe that overall there is a decline, not a rise, in the intelligence in the population.

Certainly debate about the Flynn effect, or the Lynn effect (after Richard Lynn) which is effectively the opposite, has stimulated both popular and academic debate into the definition and measurement of intelligence, particularly in educational, but also work, settings. Governments, parents and teachers are also interested in techniques which may 'boost' the intelligence of children so that they cope better with life. It has also had the effect of making all ability test publishers look carefully at their norms and meant that they seem required to partake in the expensive, but very essential, business of regularly 'renorming' their tests.

the condensed idea
Everyone seems to be getting smarter

19 Multiple intelligences

'It is undeniable that a gift for mathematics is one of the most specialised talents and that mathematicians as a class are not particularly distinguished for general ability or adversity.'
G.H. Hardy, 1940

One or many? Is intelligence all 'one thing' or made up of different intelligences? Since the 1920s psychologists have talked about 'social intelligences' which are about social rather than academic competencies.

Lumpers and splitters 'Lumpers' stress the concept 'g' (general intelligence) while 'splitters' argue that intelligence is made up of very different specific abilities not closely related. Lumpers point to the evidence which suggests that when individuals are given a range of different tests of ability (verbal reasoning, spatial intelligence, memory) they correlate highly. That is, bright people tend to do well on all of them; average people average; and less bright people poorly. Splitters point to many individual cases of people with great skills in one area but poor abilities in others.

Most academic psychologists are lumpers, believing that the extensive available evidence points to the fact that people tend to score similarly on very different tests. Indeed this is the assumption underlying conventional test measurement.

What tests measure IQ tests vary in all sorts of dimensions: some involve reasoning, others memory; some knowledge, others rule application. They test knowledge of words, numbers, shapes, recall and the explanation of practical actions. The question then is what is the

timeline

1904	1981
Spearman and general intelligence factor (g)	Jensen, *Straight Talk about Mental Tests*

correlation between test scores based on a very large sample. The answer tends to support the believers in general intelligence: the lumpers. All correlations are positive: some as high as 0.8 with an average 0.5. This means despite great variability in the tests, people who score well on one test tend to score well on all the others.

However, these correlations are done on large groups and it is perfectly possible to have individuals who are less consistent, scoring very highly on some tests but poorly on others. Second, inevitably some tests correlate more highly than others to form identifiable clusters. If scores on these clusters are correlated, then scores are even higher. Test-takers then do very well, pretty average or poorly on them all. The results point to a general mental ability or capacity which may be labelled intelligence or cognitive ability. This has been observed in at least 400 studies.

> **To judge well, to comprehend well, to reason well. These are the essential activities of intelligence.**
>
> **A. Binet and T. Simon, 1916**

Fluid and crystallized Psychologists argue that you can measure ability at different levels. Thus one may have a very specific general knowledge test like completing a crossword, which is part of what psychologists called *crystallized intelligence*, which in turn is part of general intelligence. Equally, one can measure abstract problem-solving as in Sudoku, which measures *fluid intelligence* or efficient problem-solving. The implication is that the more varied tests we give to an individual, the better because we get a clearer, more reliable reading of their specific level of intelligence.

Multiple intelligences The concept of multiple intelligence has flourished since Howard Gardner (1983) defined intelligence as 'the ability to solve problems or to create products that are valued within one or more cultural settings' and specified seven intelligences. He argued that *linguistic/verbal* and *logical/mathematical* are those typically valued in educational settings. Linguistic intelligence involves sensitivity to the spoken and written language and the ability to learn languages. Logical/mathematical intelligence involves the capacity to analyse problems logically, solve maths problems and investigate issues scientifically. These two types of intelligence dominate intelligence tests.

1983	1985	1999
Gardner, *Frames of Mind*	Sternberg, *Beyond IQ*	Gardner, *Intelligence Reframed*

Three other multiple intelligences are arts-based: *musical* intelligence, which refers to skill in the performance, composition and appreciation of musical patterns; *bodily kinaesthetic* intelligence, which is based on the use of the whole or parts of the body to solve problems or to fashion products; and *spatial* intelligence, which is the ability to recognize and manipulate patterns in space.

There are also two personal intelligences: *interpersonal* intelligence, which is the capacity to understand the intentions, motivations and desires of other people and to work effectively with them; and *intrapersonal* intelligence, which is the capacity to understand oneself and to use this information effectively in regulating one's life.

> ‘You only have to attack the IQ to become famous and popular; however nonsensical the attack, and however weak the alleged evidence for your own systems.’
>
> Hans Eysenck, 1998

Three more In his later book (*Intelligence Reframed*, 1999) Gardner defines intelligence as a 'bio-psychological potential to process information that can be activated in a cultural setting to solve problems or create products that are of value in a culture'. In this book, he introduces three candidate new intelligences. However, he only added one new intelligence, namely *naturalistic* intelligence, which is expertise in the recognition and classification of the numerous species – the flora and fauna – of one's environment. It is the capacity of taxonomization: to recognize members of a group, to distinguish among members of a species and to chart out the relations, formally or informally, among several species. The other two that were rejected as not intelligences were *spiritual* and *existential* intelligence.

Practical intelligence Yet another multidimensional model is known as the 'triarchic' theory of 'successful' intelligence of Robert Sternberg. This posits that human intelligence comprises three aspects, that is, *componential*, *experiential* and *contextual*. The componential aspect refers to a person's ability to learn new things, to think analytically and to solve problems. This aspect of intelligence is manifested through better performance on standard intelligence tests, which require general knowledge and ability in areas such as arithmetic and vocabulary. The experiential aspect refers to a person's ability to combine different experiences in unique and creative ways. It concerns original thinking and creativity in both the arts and the sciences. Finally, the contextual aspect refers to a person's ability to deal with practical aspects of the environment

Business intelligence

Do you need special abilities to be successful at work? Most people think cognitive or academic IQ and emotional intelligence would be enough. However, some psychologists have come up with various other special abilities, inevitably more controversial.

Political IQ is the ability to gain resources through exercising political power in situations where ambiguity and account-ability levels allow for a shaping of attitudes and images.

Business IQ is knowledge of how things are done via policies, procedures, planning processes and audits. It is, in effect, an understanding of the official formal rules of the organization and the ability to get things done in a specific organizational context.

Socio-cultural IQ is really cultural knowledge and ability to translate or integrate specific cues about culture. It is about the recognition and understanding of corporate norms, motives and labour.

Network IQ is essentially about inter-organizational management, and getting things done through other units.

Organizational IQ is about a detailed and accurate understanding of how to 'get things done' in the organization.

Once again, although this idea is immensely appealing to consultants and managers themselves, it is essentially misleading to label these 'intelligences'. It would be more sensible, however, to call these competencies that can be largely learnt.

and to adapt to new and changing contexts. This aspect of intelligence resembles what lay people sometimes refer to as 'street smartness'.

Enthusiasm for multiple intelligence has led to the proliferation of 'discoveries' of new intelligences. Hence 'sexual intelligence' is supposedly about mate selection. The problem for the multiple intelligence position lies in not being able to prove that these new 'intelligences' are in fact intelligences as opposed to learnt skills or personality factors and, more importantly, where they are independent of one another. It is possible to test the underlying assumption of whether multiple intelligences are related (correlated) or really independent of each other. In fact the data show the opposite and provide support for the general mental ability camp.

the condensed idea
There are different types of intelligence

20 Cognitive differences

Political correctness means you have to be courageous, naïve or stupid to talk about sex differences in intelligence or, indeed, sex differences in anything. Many people want to believe that men and women are equal not only in potential but also ability. They argue that even if there are small differences, they should not be explored or explained because of the divisive effect that it has on both sexes. 'Don't go there', researchers have been warned.

To discuss, believe in, and attempt to explain difference between different groups of human beings soon becomes ideological. It inevitably appears associated with ideas of nature–nurture, which is then associated with left-vs right-wing politics. Over the past century there have been periods where both the 'difference' and 'non-difference' views occurred. The growth of environmentalism and feminism from the 1960s onwards perpetuated the idea that any observable differences between the sexes were the result of socialization/learning. However, the pendulum from the 1990s onwards swung the other way towards a more biological and evolutionary perspective which recognized and 'explained' sex difference.

> ‘Over the past ten years, for the first time, intelligence has become socially correct for girls.’
>
> Tom Wolfe, 1987

Sex vs gender Psychologists have distinguished between *sexual identity* (based on biological sex), *gender identity* (based on awareness of sex), *sex role* (expectations of how people of one sex should behave) and *sex-typed behaviour* (behaviour a culture prescribes and proscribes for that gender).

timeline

1928	1972
British women first get the vote	Money, *Man and Woman, Boy and Girl*

Differences throughout life There really are recognized sex differences at all stages at life. So in infancy we know boys are more active and spend more time awake; girls are more physically developed and co-ordinated; girls show right-hand preference at five months (not boys); girls have better hearing and are more vocal; girls make more eye contact and are more interested in social and emotional stimuli; boys are more interested in things and systems.

In the pre-school period we know boys are more interested in block-building and vehicles; girls prefer doll play, artwork and domestic activities; boys like rough-and-tumble play; girls are more sensitive and sedentary; boys show narrow interests, girls a wider range, including boy-typical activities (asymmetrical sex-typing). Gender segregation (same-sex playgroups) appears for both boys and girls. Boys' groups are larger and more concerned with dominance issues; girls play in groups of two or three and are more sharing and concerned with fairness.

Girls develop larger vocabularies, use more complex linguistic constructions, enunciate and read better. Boys are less com-municative and use language instrumentally (to get what they want); males suffer from bilingual development (e.g. memory deficit) while females seem unimpaired.

> **The great and almost only comfort about being a woman is that one can always pretend to be more stupid than one is and no one is surprised.**
>
> **Freya Stark, 1970**

Boys on average are better at mathematical reasoning, dart-throwing and finding geometric forms in complex patterns and rotating objects. Girls are better at remembering displaced objects, recalling stories, and precision tasks calling for good motor co-ordination.

Boys say any failure they experience is down to lack of effort while often girls put their own failures down to lack of ability. Girls show more concern for feelings of others and are generally better at 'mind-reading'. Boys are more affected by bereavement, separation, maternal depression, etc., but inclined to deny loss or sorrow.

Of course these are all based on aggregated averages and cannot explain individual differences.

1974	**1975**	**2003**
Sandra Bem introduced the concept of androgyny	Sex Discrimination Act introduced into Britain	Baron-Cohen, *The Essential Difference*

Six positions on sex differences in IQ

1. Intelligence cannot be accurately measured and therefore it is difficult to prove or disprove the existence of sex difference. This view emerges every so often, usually perpetuated by educators, journalists or politicians who are ideologically opposed to testing.

2. There are no differences at all for one of two reasons. Firstly, there are no good evolutionary or environmental theories or reasons to suppose there are. Secondly, the early tests were so developed to show no difference. That is, subtests were included and excluded so that neither sex was advantaged or disadvantaged.

3. There are no mean or average differences between the sexes but there are differences at the extremes. Thus men tend to be over-represented at both the extremes of the bell curve (see Chapter 17). The most brilliant are men and so are the most challenged, meaning the average is the same but the distribution is wider for men.

4. There are numerous, demonstrable and replicable sex differences in a whole range of abilities that make up overall intelligence. They occur for an evolutionary explicable reason.

5. Sex differences that do emerge are not real. They occur for three reasons. Girls are taught humility and males hubris, and this social message leads them to approach tests differently. Next, it is less of a social requirement (particularly in mate selection) for girls to be intelligent so they invest less in education and skill development. Finally, females are less emotionally stable than males and thus anxiety reflects their test performance. So any differences that emerge do not reflect underlying reality.

6. There are real differences between the sexes, with males having a four- to eight-point advantage, which becomes noticeable after the age of 15. Before adolescence, females in fact have an advantage. The difference between the sexes is greatest for spatial intelligence. The difference is reflected in the brain size difference (corrected for body size) between men and women. Further, this 'real' difference 'explains' male superiority in arts, business, education and science.

There is a difference There are those who say that sex difference in intelligence is important and real. They tend to opt for five arguments.

- Similar differences are observed across time, culture and species (hence unlikely to be learned).

- Specific differences are predictable on the basis of evolutionary specialization (hunter/warrior vs gatherer/nurse/educator).
- Brain differences are established by pre-natal sex hormones; later on, hormones affect ability profiles (e.g. spatial suppressed by oestrogen, HRT maintains verbal memory).
- Sex-typed activity appears before gender-role awareness. At age 2, girls talk better, boys are better at construction tasks. This is not learned.
- Environmental effects (e.g. expectations, experience training) are minimal. They may exaggerate (or perhaps reduce) differences.

Nature or nurture Those who refute the idea of sex differences, however, accept the possibility of gender differences, which they argue are totally learnt. It is argued that they are learnt in every culture and hence there are noticeable cultural differences. Further, changes in how we think about culture lead to changes in gender differences.

In most cultures males are considered to be instrumental (assertive, competitive, independent) and females expressive (co-operative, sensitive, supportive). But not in all. The argument is that certain cultural differences may have originated in biological differences but that social factors have overridden this. Biology is not destiny. The media have been accused of strongly influencing gender role development.

Over the past 30–40 years various theories as to how gender differences occur have been put forward. *Social learning theory* argues that children learn appropriate sex role behaviour by three types of learning at certain crucial stages in their life: direct teaching, imitation and observatory learning. *Gender schema theory* suggests that children are taught to develop a clear set of beliefs or ideas or constructs called schema about gender which helps them interpret and behave in the world.

‘A woman especially, if she have the misfortune of knowing anything, should conceal it as well as she can.’

Jane Austen,
Northanger Abbey, 1803

People can be strongly masculine or feminine or both (androgynous) or neither (undifferentiated) in their role behaviour. For a long period it was thought that androgyny was the 'best' or 'healthiest' compromise. This has emerged today as the concept of the 'meterosexual' person.

the condensed idea
Men and women think differently

21 The Rorschach inkblot test

If people are unwilling or unable to discuss their innermost fears, hopes and aims, could we find these out by asking them what they see in pictures? Could they 'project' their unacceptable, perhaps forbidden, dreams and fantasies into stories or pictures? The idea, common in popular psychology, is that choices and descriptions 'tell you a lot about a person'. But it was a Swiss psychologist, Hermann Rorschach, who devised a famous test more than 80 years ago. The idea had been suggested in 1895 by Binet, the person later to become famous for the first IQ test.

The most well known version of the test comprises ten separate cards of symmetrical inkblots, half coloured, half monochrome. They were found to show the shapes that were most diagnostic. The tester gives the person a card at a time and asks them to say what they see. This is repeated. Testers note what is said, how long the person spends looking at each card, which way up they hold it, etc.

Scoring the test Strictly the orthodox administration of the test goes through four phases. The performance phase requires the testee to say spontaneously what they see on each card. Everything said should be written down. The second is the inquiry phase, which is more structured. The tester tries to enquire about two things and goes back over each card. He or she asks about location and detail. The tester looks at whether the testee is looking at the inkblot as a whole or, if not, which parts drew their attention. An enquiry is also

> **'If subjects describe any of the Rorschach inkblots as an inkblot this is regarded as a defensive response.'**
>
> **Paul Kline, 1993**

timeline

1921	1939
Rorschach, *Psychodiagnostik*	New concept of projective techniques

made about what made the inkblot resemble the object the testee saw: form, movement, shading, colour.

The third stage is called the analogy phase, where the tester probes into the choices made by the testee and wonders what they could mean or indicate. In the final testing-the-limits-phase, the tester offers other 'popular' perceptions and wonders aloud if the testee can see those as well.

Then the interpretation phase begins. This is surprisingly elaborate and has a number of letters that scorers use to indicate various phenomena. So M refers to imagination and the extent to which the readings are 'peopled'. K refers to anxiety and is picked up by colour and movement. D lets the tester know how much common sense the person has. S refers to the testee's oppositional tendencies and this is picked up by interpreting the white space or very small details. The scoring system can easily look like a strange mixture between a cookbook and a magic book.

The following are typical interpretations.

Response	Interpretation
Frequent responses to small, clearly defined parts of the inkblot patterns	Obsessional personality with perfectionism and meticulousness
Frequently sees moving animals	Impulsive, demanding immediate gratification
Reponses often purely determined by colour (alone)	Emotionally uncontrolled, explosive
Often sees small, passive animals	Passive, dependent personality and attitudes
Tendency to see maps	Guarded and evasive
Often sees facial masks	Reluctant to show the real self

There are different expert systems to score this test but many look at different aspects of the cards. The idea is to do a diagnosis or paint a profile of the real individual. One argument is that people can't or won't accurately talk about their real motives, hopes and ambitions. They can't either because they do not have insight into their powerful, deep unconscious motives or they are simply unable to articulate them. Or people will not

1943
Thematic Apperception Test

1954
The most famous Rorschach scoring method introduced

2004
Savage attack by A. Paul in *The Cult of Personality*

really tell the truth about their deepest desires, hopes and ambitions. Psychologists worry about two forms of dissimulation or lying: impression management, which is saying only the thing about oneself that causes a positive impression; and self-deception, where people think they are actually telling the truth about themselves while this is clearly not the case. Projective techniques like the inkblot analysis supposedly overcome these problems.

The inkblot tests are not the only *projective techniques* in psychology. What they have in common is that they give a person a stimulus (usually a picture; it could be a sound, or smell) and then encourage them to project into or onto it their immediate, innermost and intense thoughts, feelings and desires. They say how they react to an ambiguous stimulus. The more unclear, ambiguous or vague the stimulus, the more the person projects themselves onto it.

Five categories of projective tests

Inkblot or abstract pictures These can be constructed very simply by dropping a large 'blob' of wet ink on the middle of a page, folding it in half and then looking at the resultant pattern.

Sounds People listen to sounds (songs, baby crying, car crashing) or music and describe how they react.

Sentence completion People complete the following: 'I wish I had never . . .', 'I am . . .',

'My greatest fear is . . .', 'I am rather proud about . . .'.

Free drawing People are asked to draw certain objects (a house, a car, a parent) and then answer questions about them.

Solid objects The person is asked to play with, construct or manoeuvre a solid object (doll, block, sand) while describing what they are doing.

The projective hypothesis has stayed alive in psychology for a long time, partly because psychologists seem less good at uncovering people's motivations, particularly their motivations to be successful and achieve. Thus David McClelland, who worked extensively with the second most famous projective test in psychology (Thematic Apperception Test, which is a series of drawings rather than inkblots), claimed that it uncovered three of the most important and fundamental of all drives or needs. They are the need for achievement, power and affiliation. The idea is that people tell stories about these pictures which give accurate insights into these drives which they cannot talk about.

Criticisms of the tests There are four – some think devastating – objections to the use of these tests on scientific grounds. Firstly, they are unreliable because different experts or scores come up with quite different interpretations. If the testers can't agree on the meanings, we can't get anywhere. Secondly, they are invalid because the scores don't predict anything. In short, they don't measure what they say they are measuring. Thirdly, context makes all the difference. The mood of the person, the characteristics of the tester, the setting of the test all affect results, which suggests they are picking up on trivial rather than essential, underlying factors. Fourthly, the testers can't agree on what the tests measure: attitudes, abilities, defences, motivation, deep desires. By measuring everything they may measure nothing.

> **In short there is no single, inevitable meaning attached to a given response; all things are relative and interpretation requires considerable training and experience.**
>
> **E.J. Phares, 1984**

So why do these tests still get used? Is it lazy journalists, charlatan psychologists or naïve managers who use these (discredited) tests? Why are they still used despite limitations?

- They provide often unique and intriguing data relatively easily that cannot be obtained as cheaply, quickly and easily elsewhere.
- Skilled and trained practitioners seem able to obtain impressive, reliable and insightful findings which they can't get from other tests or interviews.
- The richness of the data makes other test data often look crude, colourless and constipated.
- They can complement and confirm other findings and ideas.

So, after nearly 100 years, some psychologists still use the inkblots to try to understand personality, but it certainly has become a less acceptable method to those concerned with developing valid and reliable methods.

the condensed idea
Can inkblots help understand personality?

22 Detecting lies

The idea of having a reliable, physiologically-based way of catching liars has always appealed to people – more so in the 20th century with its love of science fiction. A lie detector is a physical countermeasure that attempts to detect dissimilation. Some have tried pharmacological or truth-drug methods with limited success.

Getting to the truth The earliest records of quasi-lie detectors can be found in ancient Hindu and medieval Church methods of finding the truth. Suspects were asked to chew various substances and then spit them out. The ease of spitting and glutinousness of the spittle reflected guilt. What these people had observed was that fear leads to saliva diminishing in volume and becoming viscous. Today we would say that anxiety influences the activity of the autonomic nervous system that controls salivation.

In the 19th century various scientists tried measuring other supposed physical concomitants of fear. Various instruments were used whilst investigating suspects, including the 'plethysmograph', which recorded pulse and blood pressure in a limb, finger trembling, reaction time, word association and so on.

The history of the polygraph The lie detector, or polygraph, was devised in the 1930s but from the mid-1970s various psychologists started serious investigations into the lie detector and all condemned it. In 1988 the Polygraph Protection Act prohibited US employers from requiring or requesting that employees be polygraphed. However, in half of American states lie detector evidence can still be admitted. Polygraphs are now used throughout the world from Canada to Thailand, Israel to Taiwan, though their use is limited.

timeline

1938	1960s
Marston, *The Lie Detector Test*	Lie detectors used widely in business

The validity of the lie detector To be acceptable as a test a lie detector must minimally fulfil a number of criteria. Firstly, there must be a standardized method of administration, which is fully described, clear and repeatable. Secondly, there must be objective scoring. Thirdly, there must be external valid criteria – it must always and accurately be shown to differentiate between truth and lies.

Researchers say evaluation must take into consideration four factors:

- the difference between *accuracy* and *utility* – how the polygraph might be useful even if it isn't accurate

How polygraphs work

The polygraph measures autonomic nervous system activity by sensors attached to different parts of the body: chest, stomach, fingers. These sensors measure changes in breathing (depth and rate), cardiac activity (blood pressure) and perspiration. It is also possible to measure brain electrical activity. The indicators only show physiological changes, usually induced by emotion. The machine amplifies signals picked up from sensors placed at specific parts of the body. It detects not lies, but physical changes that are the results of specific emotions (fear, anger, guilt) – but which of these is not clear. People are asked 'hot' or relevant questions as well as 'cool' or control questions. The assumption is that for innocent people there is no physical difference in the way they respond to relevant and control questions. But some people are more reactive than others.

Drugs can be used to suppress autonomic nervous system activity and make any physiological recording inconclusive. More worryingly, people can be trained to defeat the test with a range of techniques. Tests would therefore not only be highly unreliable but counterproductive: alienating and misclassifying the innocent and letting the guilty get away scot-free.

The lie-detector remains used in three different contexts: criminal investigations, security vetting and personnel selection. Some argue the base rate of liars is too low ever to be accurate. Others suggest that the test causes a poor impression. However, some argue that taking the test or threatening to have to take it leads people to admitting important things they otherwise would not admit. Thus a test can have utility even without accuracy.

1988	**2000**	**2001**
USA passes the Polygraph Protection Act	Vrij, *Detecting Lies and Deceit*	Still over one million polygraph tests done annually in the US

Emotional 'leakage'

Many of the clues about lying are about looking for emotional and verbal cues (spoken language).

- *Response latency*, or the time elapsing between the end of a question and the beginning of their response. Liars take longer.

- *Frequency and length of pauses*, or the number of times people seem uncertain of what to say or what they have been saying.

- *Linguistic distance* – not saying 'I', 'he', 'she', but talking in the abstract even when recalling incidents in which they were involved.

- *Speech errors* – hesitating, Freudian slips, over-use of 'ums' and 'errs' and sudden changes in speed of talking.

- *Slow but uneven speech* – as they try to think while speaking but get caught out. It is the change in pace as a function of a particular question that gives a clue that something is not right.

- *Too eager to fill silences* – to keep talking when it is unnecessary. Liars overcompensate and seem uncomfortable with what are often quite short pauses.

- *Too many 'pitch raises'* – that is, instead of the pitch dropping at the end of a reply it rises like a question. It may sound like 'Do you believe me now?'

- *A loss of resonance in the voice* – it becomes flatter, less deep, more monotonous.

There are also some non-verbal cues.

- *Squirming* – shifting around too much in the chair. Shown by numerous and unusual head, leg, foot and trunk movements.

- *Having too much eye contact*, as liars tend to overcompensate.

- *Micro-expression*, or flickers of expressions (of surprise, hurt, anger) – difficult to see unless frames are frozen.

- *An increase in comfort gestures* – self-touching the face and upper body.

- *Changes in facial expression*, particularly smiling, blinking and eye-gaze patterns.

> ❝ . . . a lie which is all a lie maybe met and fought with outright. But a lie which is part a truth is a harder matter to fight. ❞
>
> **Alfred Lord Tennyson, 1859**

> **The face may contain many different clues to deceit: micros (expressions), squelched expressions, leakage in the reliable facial muscles, blinking, pupil dilation, tearing, blushing and blanching, asymmetry, mistakes in timing, mistakes in location, and false smiles. Some of these clues provide leakage, betraying concealed information; others provide deception clues indicating that something is being concealed but not what; and others mark an expression to be false.**
>
> **Paul Ekman, 1976**

- the quest for *ground truth* – how hard it is to determine the accuracy of the polygraph without being absolutely certain who the liars are
- the *base rate of lying* – how a very accurate test can produce many mistakes when the group of suspects includes very few liars
- *deterring lying* – how the threat of being examined might inhibit some from lying, even if the examination procedure is faulty.

Under experimental conditions people get misclassified: a surprisingly high percentage of the guilty are thought innocent and vice versa. The question is, why and how much? And with what consequences? Misclassification may be 2–10 per cent. It is the consequences of judging anxious, truthful people to be liars and psychopathic liars as telling the truth that have led governments and learned societies to ban or at least argue against the use of the lie detector.

Beating the machine Can you beat the lie detector? Essentially there are two ways of doing this: physical or mental. Physical measures may involve self-inflicted pain (biting the tongue, keeping a drawing pin hidden in a shoe; tensing and releasing muscles). Mental methods may include backward counting or trying even to have erotic thoughts or fantasies. The former are meant to give real, dramatic but misleading readings.

the condensed idea
Lie detectors can be used and misused

23 Authoritarian personality

What kind of people accepted Nazi ideology and took part in the Holocaust? What drives people to be so certain about believing they are right and everybody else is wrong? Why can they be so fundamentalistic about so many issues?

Personality and Nazism After the Second World War a group of American-based social scientists, led by Theodor Adorno, posed this question. It resulted in a book called *The Authoritarian Personality*, published in 1950.

Their theory focused on the individual as a cause of social evils. The basic argument went as follows. Parents bring about authoritarianism by frequently and seriously punishing and shaming their children for even minor offences. This makes the children hostile to their parents and all authority figures and those in power. However, the child does not consciously acknowledge this aggression because it may cause yet more punishment. Also they are dependent on their parents, whom they are supposed to love. So, the argument goes, their repressed antagonism is displaced and projected onto weaker members of society. Authoritarians are nearly always ethnocentric in that they have a certain, simple and unshakable belief in the superiority of their own racial, cultural and ethnic group, with a powerful disdain for all those in other groups. This can easily lead to brutality, aggression and naked, open prejudice.

While the idea took hold, it has been criticized, both because many other factors lead to the development of authoritarian thinking and behaviour but also because prejudiced behaviour is shaped by others for powerful situational factors (see Chapters 24 and 25).

timeline

1950	1954
Adorno and colleagues, *The Authoritarian Personality*	Eysenck, *The Psychology of Politics*

Authoritarians have been shown to avoid situations that involve any sort of ambiguity or uncertainty, and are reluctant to believe that 'good people' possess both good and bad attributes. However, they often appear less interested in political affairs, participate less in political and community activities, and tend to prefer strong leaders.

Measuring authoritarianism There are a number of measures of authoritarianism; the best known (and hence the most widely used) is the California F scale, first published in *The Authoritarian Personality*,

The California F scale

Conventionalism Rigid adherence to conventional middle-class values. ('Obedience and respect for authority are the most important virtues children should learn.')

Authoritarian submission Uncritical acceptance of authority. ('Young people sometimes get rebellious ideas, but as they grow up they ought to get over them and settle down.')

Authoritarian aggression A tendency to condemn anyone who violates conventional norms. ('A person who has bad manners, habits and breeding can hardly expect to get along with decent people.')

Sex Exaggerated concern for proper sexual conduct. ('Homosexuals are hardly better than criminals and ought to be severely punished.')

Anti-intraception Rejection of weakness or sentimentality. ('The businessman and the manufacturer are much more important to society than the artist and professor.')

Superstition and stereotypy Belief in mystical determinants of action and rigid, categorical thinking. ('Some day it will probably be shown that astrology can explain a lot of things.')

Power and toughness Preoccupation with dominance over others. ('No weakness or difficulty can hold us back if we have enough willpower.')

Destructiveness and cynicism A generalized feeling of hostility and anger. ('Human nature being what it is, there will always be war and conflict.')

Projectivity A tendency to project inner emotions and impulses outward. ('Most people don't realize how much our lives are controlled by plots hatched in secret places.')

1960	1973	1981
Rokeach, *The Open and Closed Mind*	Wilson, *The Psychology of Conservatism*	Altmeyer, *Right-Wing Authoritarianism*

which attempts to measure prejudice and rigid thinking. The box identifies nine factors and statements reflecting each part of the scale.

Ethnocentrism and ambiguity avoidance There are various different concepts related to that of authoritarianism. These include conservatism, dogmatism and ethnocentrism. Some focus on thinking style, others on prejudice. Most argue that this 'attitudinal syndrome', rather than a personality trait, occurs for both genetic/hereditary and environmental factors. At the core of the theories is the idea of a generalized susceptibility to experience anxiety and threat when confronted by ambiguity or uncertainty.

> **Some system of authority is a requirement of all communal living, and it is only the man dwelling in isolation who is not forced to respond, through defiance or submission, to the commands of others.**
> **Stanley Milgram, 1974**

Thus for various reasons – ability and personality, early life and current circumstances – authoritarians feel inferior and insecure and fearful of lack of clarity. Therefore, their motivation is to avoid uncertainty. Authoritarians dislike anything or anybody that advocates complexity, innovation, novelty, risk or change. They tend to dislike conflict and decision-making and subjugate their personal feelings and needs to external authorities. They obey the rules, norms, conventions and, more importantly, they insist others do, too.

So conservatives and authoritarians get obsessed by ordering and controlling their internal and external worlds. They like simplistic, rigid and inflexible duties, laws, morals, obligations and rules. This affects everything from their choice of art to how they vote.

Closed-minded, dogmatic, authoritarian people are characterized by three things: a strong desire to reject all ideas opposed to their own; a low degree of connectedness among various beliefs; many more complex and positive ideas about things/issues they do believe in as opposed to those they don't believe in.

Right-wing authoritarianism The latest work in this area is exclusively on right-wing authoritarianism (RWA). The distinction is made because it is recognized that left-wing people like Stalinists and Trotskyists can equally be authoritarian. The idea is that RWA is made of up three attitudinal and behavioural clusters. The first is total submission to established authorities; the second, generalized aggression to all 'enemies' of those authorities; and the third, blind adherence to established social norms

Dogmatism

Closed-mindedness and dogmatism are concepts closely related to authoritarianism. It is not a matter of intelligence, but open-minded people do solve questions more quickly and they seem able to synthesize information more quickly into new ideas. That is why they seem happier with novel, difficult and strange problems. Closed-minded people tend to get aggressive or withdraw when faced by novel ideas. There are many dogmatized questionnaires. Here are some statements from them.

- In this complicated world of ours the only way we can know what's going on is to rely on leaders or experts who can be trusted.

- My blood boils whenever a person stubbornly refuses to admit he's wrong.

- There are two kinds of people in this world: those who are for the truth and those who are against the truth.

- Most people just don't know what's good for them.

- Of all the different philosophies which exist in this world there is probably only one which is correct.

- Most of the ideas which get printed nowadays aren't worth the paper they're printed on.

and conventions. So those with strong RWA beliefs are absolutists, bullies, dogmatists, hypocrites and zealots. They are enthusiastic advocates of punishment of all kinds and dubious about liberals and libertarianism. They are uncritical of all they stand for, and are at times inconsistent and hold contradictory ideas. They are noticeably open to the criticism of holding double standards but simultaneously self-righteous and not at all humble or self-critical.

Authoritarians are found in all walks of life, though they do get attracted to jobs and religions that concur with their particular values. They would be more likely to describe themselves as 'right-thinking', moral, rational, polite and honest than authoritarian. However, their political and religious beliefs will make them relatively easy to detect.

the condensed idea
Are dictators born or bred?

24 Obedience to authority

'The social psychology of this century reveals a major lesson: often it is not so much the kind of person that a person is as the kind of situation in which he finds himself that determines how he will act.' Stanley Milgram, 1974

When Adolf Eichmann was tried for his part in the Holocaust, his defence was that he was 'only obeying orders'. The American soldiers at My Lai in Vietnam who followed Lt Calley's orders said likewise. It is easy to argue that insane men during wartime perform such acts but that it would never happen to people like you and me. But psychologists have shown that it can and does.

Conformity vs obedience

Why do people comply, conform and obey the orders of others? Obedience and conformity (Chapter 25) are not the same, and differ in the following ways:

- **Explicitness** In obedience the prescription for action (an order) is explicit, whereas in conformity the requirement of going along with the group is implicit.

- **Hierarchy** Conformity regulates the behaviour of equal-status subjects whereas obedience links one status to another.

- **Imitation** Conformity is imitation, obedience is not.

- **Voluntarism** Because conformity is a response to implicit pressure, the subject interprets his/her own behaviour as voluntary. However, the obedience situation is publicly defined as one devoid of voluntarism and thus the subject can fall back on the public definition of the situation as the full explanation of his/her action.

timeline

1965	1968
Milgram's first studies in the area	My Lai massacre in Vietnam

The famous study Perhaps the most dramatic experiment in psychology in the 20th century was that of Stanley Milgram (1974), whose book caused a storm. What the study showed was that nice, normal, middle-class Americans were prepared to shock to death an innocent man who wasn't too hot on memorizing paired words.

Volunteers were told they were to take part in an experiment on human learning. Their particular job was to consist of delivering electric shocks to a learner each time he made an error in learning associations between paired words. The volunteers saw their 'fellow volunteer' strapped into a chair; they saw electrode paste and electrodes attached to his arm. In some cases, they heard their 'pupil' (the 'learner') tell the experimenter that he had a slight heart condition, but the experimenter reassured them that although the shocks might be painful, they would cause no permanent tissue damage.

All the good of which humanity is capable is comprised in obedience.

John Stuart Mill, 1859

The experimenter conducted the 'teacher' (the naïve volunteer) to another room and showed him/her the machine with which he/she was to deliver the 'punishment'. It was an impressive-looking device with switches marked from 15 to 450 volts in 15-volt increments. Below the numerical labels were others characterizing the shocks. These ranged from 'SLIGHT SHOCK' at the low end to 'INTENSE SHOCK' in the middle, through 'DANGER: SEVERE SHOCK', and finally to a simple, stark 'XXX' beneath the last two switches.

The teacher was to give the learner a 15-volt shock for his first wrong answer, and was to shock him again every time he made a mistake. The teacher was to increase his punishment one shock level (15 volts) for every wrong answer. The learner was in fact a friend of the experimenter; the only real shock delivered was the sample shock given to the teacher. But the teacher didn't know this.

The sessions began innocuously enough: the learner got some of the pairs right, but he soon made an error and was 'given' a mild 15-volt shock. Until 75-volts, the teacher had no indication that he/she was causing the learner much pain. But at 75 volts, the learner grunted in pain. The teacher could

1974	2000	2007
Milgram, *Obedience to Authority*	Experiments repeated with similar effects	Zimbardo, *The Lucifer Effect*

hear the grunt through the wall separating them. At 120 volts, the learner shouted to the experimenter that the shocks were becoming painful. At 150 volts, the learner screamed, 'Experimenter get me out of here! I won't be in the experiment any more!' The learner continued to cry out in pain, with his cries increasing in intensity, becoming agonized screams once the shocks reached 270 volts. The experimenter and teacher were now strictly speaking engaged in torture.

Torture and death At 300 volts, the learner shouted in desperation that he would no longer respond to the word pairs. The experimenter – our, cold, steely authority figure – matter-of-factly informed the volunteer to treat 'no response' as if it were an error, and to go on administering shock. From this point on, the volunteer heard no more from the learner; he or she did not know whether the learner was alive. The volunteer could certainly see that the torture had become pointless, whatever else was true: because the learner was no longer answering, he was surely no longer taking part in a learning experiment. When the volunteer reached the end of the shock board, he or she was told to continue using the last lever for all subsequent 'mistakes'. The volunteers were, of course, physically free to leave the experiment, to relieve the victim's suffering; the victim was strapped in, but nothing barred the subject's escape.

> **❛Never command unless you mean to be obeyed.❜**
>
> **Anon**

Twenty-six of the 40 male volunteers who took part in the experiment continued to the end; the same number of women, 26 out of 40, continued to the end. The fully obedient subjects stopped administering the 450-volt shocks to the victim only when the experimenter told them to stop.

Further studies The study was replicated, changing various features so that their effect on obedience could be observed. The further study showed the following:

- *Proximity to victim* – subjects obey more, the closer they are to a suffering victim.
- *Proximity to authority* – subjects obey less, the further away the authority who gives the command is.
- *Institutional setting* – conducting the experiments in a run-down office building reduced obedience only slightly.
- *Conformity pressures* – obedient peers increase subjects' obedience; rebellious peers greatly reduce obedience.

- *Role of person giving commands* – people obey others most when those others are perceived to be legitimate authorities; in Milgram's studies, subjects generally obeyed the experimenter but did not obey other subjects.
- *Personality traits* – in Milgram's studies, assessed traits correlated weakly with obedience.
- *Cultural difference* – cross-cultural replication shows some variation across cultures, but obedience tends to be high regardless of culture.
- *Attitudinal and ideological factors* – religious people are more likely to obey in Milgram-type experiments.

Obedience in the Milgram experiment is not a matter of the volunteers giving over their will to the experimenter; rather, it is a matter of the experimenter persuading them that they have a moral obligation to continue. The 'moral' aspect of the experimenter–volunteer relationship is sustained in part by the impersonal nature of the experimenter's behaviour.

Researchers have turned their attention to understanding and teaching how and why certain people resist. The Milgram experiment remains perhaps the most famous in the whole of psychology and it is not difficult to see why.

Alternative explanations

Evaluation apprehension When people take part in a research project, they often feel that the investigator is evaluating them. To appear helpful and 'normal', they did whatever the experimenter asked though they would not necessarily do so in a real situation.

Subject roles Research participants may also behave differently depending on the subject role they enact when they enter the study. Some people try to fulfil the 'good subject' role by carefully following instructions and by conscientiously performing all requirements of the research. Others may adopt a bad or negative subject role: they complain that the research is trivial and uninteresting and therefore refuse to co-operate with the researcher at every turn.

Experimenter effects Demand characteristics are those features of the situation that volunteers believe demand (or require) they behave in a particular way. Milgram's experimenter was supremely 'matter of fact'.

the condensed idea
Why do we comply, conform and obey?

25 Fitting in

Sociology textbooks contain chapters on deviance; psychology textbooks on conformity. Sociologists are interested in, and puzzled by, those who rebel against, deviate from, or do not conform to, the norms and rules of society. They look at groups and societies as the 'unit of analysis'.

Psychologists who have the individual (or at most the small group) as the unit of analysis are equally puzzled by why people conform. Why do adolescents who fight not to wear a school uniform in effect all dress the same? Why do we have 'fashion victims' blindly and expensively following the crowd? What real or imaginary social pressures cause people to follow the behaviour or lead of others?

Experiments There are two famous studies in the study of conformity: one guessing in the dark; the other deciding in a situation as plain as day. One study done 80 years ago (by Muzafer Sherif) required students to sit in a totally darkened room watching only a single point of light. They were told to say when it moved, where and by how much. In fact the light was stationary. But in the room were confederates or 'stooges' of the experimenter who claimed out loud that they saw it move. What they found is that ordinary people were influenced by the confederate, tending to agree with their judgement. Eventually our 'real' judge would be convinced of the movement of the stationary light. So in ambiguous and unclear situations people tend to follow the behaviour of confident and consistent peers. We look to others to enlighten us about what is going on.

The second study was run in 1952 by a psychologist called Solomon Asch. Students, in groups of five, were asked to take part in a perceptual study.

timeline

1936
Sherif, *The Psychology of Social Norms*

1952
Asch published the most famous study

They were shown around 30 pairs of cards: one 'standard card' and one 'comparison card'. The standard card had one line and the comparison card three lines labelled A, B, C of clearly different length. You simply had to say which of the three lines was the same length as the standard. It was obvious and clear. But what the experimental participant did not know was that all other four student volunteers were confederates and he or she was put always at the end to shout out his/her answer last after hearing what they had said. They shouted out their answers: A, A, A, A . . . but A was not the (obviously) correct answer. What to say: the wrong (conformist) answer A; the correct answer B; or the other wrong (anti-conformist, incorrect) answer C?

Conformity is one side of man, uniqueness the other.
Carl Jung, 1960

Around a third of the participants were swayed to conform to the group. Some gave the right answer, but were clearly uncomfortable doing so. It was a major demonstration of conformity.

Further studies Asch's experiment was repeated many times, varying different features to see what effect they had on conformity.

- *Task difficulty and ambiguity* – the more difficult the task, or ambiguous the stimuli, the more subjects look at others as sources of information, especially in opinions and abilities that have reference to social reality.

The American ideal, after all, is that everyone should be as alike as possible.
James Baldwin, 1955

- *The nature of the stimulus* – conformity behaviour varies considerably as a function of what type of judgement people are asked to make: the more factual and clear the problem, the less the conformity that results.

- *Source certainty* – the more certain a person is of the reliability and correctness of the influence source (others making the decisions), the more likely they are to conform to it.

- *Group size* – researchers have disagreed as to whether the relationship between group size and conformity is linear (more is more powerful) or curvilinear (an optimal number of people works and after that there is

1955	1960s	1980s
First investigation of the personality of conformers	Studies on cultural differences in conformity	Conformity concepts used in selling techniques

reduced influence), though there does appear to be an optimal conformity-inducing group size.

- *Unanimity of group judgement* – the more unanimous the group judgement, the more conformity is elicited; quite small amounts of deviation within the majority lead to a large reduction in conformity responses.

- *Group composition and attraction* – cohesive groups of high status, and prestigious males, tend to elicit most conformity: the more attractive the group, the more a person is likely to be influenced by it.

- *Group acceptance* – high-status people have 'idiosyncrasy credit' and can deviate, as do very low-status or rejected group members; people of middle status usually conform most.

- *Private or public behaviour* – people tend to conform more when asked to give their judgement or to behave publicly rather than privately. Anonymity has a very powerful impact on conformity.

- *Previous success or failure of the group* – a person will conform more to a group that has a past history of success than to one that has consistently failed.

- *Consistency of the minority* – a convinced, coherent minority forming a representative subgroup of individuals can greatly influence majority opinion. It is most important that the minority is consistent in its position if it is to have any effect on the majority.

> **'Why do you have to be a nonconformist like everybody else?'**
>
> **James Thurber, 1948**

Why follow others? The fundamental question then is why do people conform? The short answer is that people want to be right and they want to be liked. They respond to informational influence and normative influence.

People look to others for clues on how to behave. What is correct etiquette? The less informed we believe ourselves to be and the more informed we believe those around us, the more we 'follow the crowd'. This seems a rational process. We also conform because we like to 'fit in'; to gain social acceptance. This is the very essence of social pressure. We do so because of our need to belong. Most of us think of ourselves as members of a social group. To be a member we need to follow the rules and norms. So social conformity helps us maintain our self-perceived, indeed actual, group membership. So at different times and in different places we respond to, or reject, group norms. Indeed we may even become anti-conformist.

Of course there are personality and cultural predictors of conformity. People with low self-confidence and more authoritarian attitude conform more. Those who are more mature and have higher *ego* strength conform less. There is also evidence of some cultural factors in conformity. Cultures that tend to be more individualistic have less pressure to conformity than collectivistic cultures. Similarly, those who are homogenous with strong religious or political ideology tend to be more conformist.

> **❝Take the tone of the company you are in.❞**
> **The Earl of Chesterfield, 1747**

gaining compliance

Politicians and parents, salespersons and teachers use various techniques to get others to comply.

'Foot-in-the-door' Ask for something very small or minor (sign a petition, get change) then ask for something bigger – the thing you really want. It works if the first request is just big enough to make people think about what they are doing and also if they believe they have full 'free will' to refuse. The idea is to get people to believe that they are helpful, so they comply to the second, greater request.

'Door-in-the face' Here you try a high-demand request ('please give me £10';

'could you lend me your car?'), but then (on refusal) you back down to a much smaller request. This turned-down concessionary and conciliatory request triggers off reciprocity. To make it work, the first request must be refused, the second request made by the same person, and the target person feel the pressure to reciprocate.

'That's not all' You make someone an offer but before they answer you increase the favourability of your proposition. Either you drop the price, increase the amount or throw in extras. This works by similar principles to those above. You are helpful and liked . . . so they are too.

the condensed idea
What will we do to conform?

26 Self-sacrifice or selfishness

Why are some people 'have-a-go-heroes', while others ignore the plight and pleas of those in danger? Why are some happy to lay down their life for their family but not their friends? Is there ever true selflessness?

On a day-to-day basis we indulge in social exchange or social economics. We give and receive reciprocally. Some people help others and volunteer to do things hoping to disguise self-interest. Some 'altruistically' volunteer in order to learn skills, enhance job prospects, gain group admission or approval, reduce guilt, boost self-esteem or express their personal values.

The Good Samaritan Is there an identifiable type of person who one many accurately describe as an altruistic personality type? One study

Helping and altruism

There is a difference between helping and altruism. The essence of the latter is that people help without any anticipation of rewards from any external sources for providing assistance.

Psychologists talk about pro-social behaviour, which is any act performed with the goal of helping another person. The motive may or may not be altruistic, which is the drive to help others even if it costs oneself. For some this means doing something entirely out of the 'goodness of one's heart' because they feel empathy for a person in a situation of need.

timeline

AD 100	**1950s**
Parable of the Good Samaritan	Post-war studies of altruistic rescuers of Jews in Nazi Germany

identified specific individuals well known for their altruistic acts. The search was to find what they had in common. It showed the most critical life history factor was a traumatic experience of early loss (such as the death of a parent) with the immediate near-simultaneous exposure to a rescuer. The study seemed to suggest that later altruism served as a way to deal with painful feelings of dependency and with feelings of anger and anxiety about loss.

We have all witnessed some cars speeding past a stranded motorist but one stopping to help. Why do some people help more than others? There is evidence of sex differences but they seem to be related to the type rather than the amount of altruism. Males predominate in chivalrous, bold, heroic pro-social behaviours; females being more nurturing or caring.

People tend to help others from their own cultural group. So we are more likely to help people from noticeably the same ethnic, religious, linguistic and demographic group than a member of another group. Cross-cultural studies have tended to show that countries with collectivistic vs individualistic cultures help more. Another finding refers to the Spanish word *simpático*, which means 'friendly', 'helpful', 'polite'. Some studies have shown that people from Spanish-speaking and Latin American countries indeed show highest altruism.

One line of research has shown the 'feel good: do good' factor. Various studies have shown that when people are in a good mood they are much more likely to help others. Give a person a small gift, play pleasant upbeat music, compliment them and they voluntarily give more help to others. However, there is also evidence for the negative-state relief hypothesis, which asserts that sometimes people who are sad and distressed help others so as to feel better and reduce their gloom. Equally, people who feel guilty have been shown to increase their helpfulness, presumably to reduce their guilt. All this means is that very temporary factors which affect our mood can really impact on our helping others in need.

The "altruist" expects reciprocation from society for himself and his closest relatives.
Andrew Marvell, 1650

Guilt, self destruction, sexual striving and conflict about homosexuality are the fundamental forces underlying generosity and altruism.
Sigmund Freud, 1930

1968
Studies of bystander intervention

1980
Dawkins, *The Selfish Gene*

1990s
Charities look at how to exploit altruism

Freudian speculations Psychoanalysts always look for deeper meanings in behaviour, particularly when they see it expressing some underlying conflict. They see the same altruistic behaviour as the manifestation of two very different drives. Some generous, helping acts occur because of identification with the 'victim'. Altruistic people identify with helpful figures in their past like parents or teachers.

But Freudians also believe that altruism can be a defence against a negative impulse: a neurotic syndrome to cope with anxiety, guilt or hostility. Thus a deprived child may become a generous giver. Instead of feeling helpless around those in need, they help therefore, being both giver and receiver.

Others may cope with their guilt about their own greed and envy by giving. Some get into debt, giving to assuage their guilt. Further and paradoxically, Freudians talk of hostility-based reaction-formation giving. Thus the giver masks an expression of aggression by being helpful.

'I'd lay down my life for two brothers or eight cousins.'

J.B.S. Haldane, 1974

Evolutionary psychology of helping A central tenet of this approach is the concept of *kin selection*. The more a person (relative) shares your genes, the more likely you are to help. Thus you ensure survival of your own genes by helping those with your genes. The biological importance rule becomes ingrained into human behaviour and is not conscious.

However, evolutionists suggest the *reciprocity norm*, which is a tit-for-tat behaviour that supposes that helping others will increase the likelihood that they help you in return. Strictly speaking this is helping rather than altruistic behaviour. However, it has been suggested that people who learn and practise the norms and cultures of society will survive best because cultures teach survival skills and co-operative behaviours. So people become genetically programmed to learn cultural norms of altruism. However, the power of evolutionary explanation to account for heroic, life-sacrificial altruism to complete strangers seems less than convincing.

Context and decisions Situational factors may be more important than personal factors. People in small towns or the countryside are more likely to offer help than city-dwellers. The *urban overload* hypothesis suggests that people living in big, crowded cities keep themselves to themselves and help others less than rural people because they are bombarded and frequently overwhelmed by stimulation of all kinds.

The longer a person has lived in an area and identifies with that community, the more he or she is likely to help. The higher the residential mobility factor, the less stable the community and the less forthcoming the help of any kind. People in communal relationships invest more in the long-term future of their community and are thus more likely to offer help.

Without a doubt the most famous and counterintuitive finding in this area is the *bystander effect*. It shows that there is no safety in numbers. In short, the *greater* the number of bystanders (or witnesses) to an emergency or situation requiring help, the *less* likely any one individual is to help.

This research has led to the development of the five-step decision model of bystander intervention. It asserts that people must go through five steps before they offer help.

- They must obviously notice the event. People who are in a hurry, talking on their mobile phone or otherwise distracted might simply not notice an emergency.

- They must interpret the scene as an emergency where help is required. Many emergencies are confusing. People look to those around them for clues. If others seem unconcerned, people are unlikely to respond. Situational ambiguity leads to misinterpretation and apathy.

- They must assume some sort of responsibility. People have to decide that it is their responsibility, not others', to help. The issue rests on their shoulders alone.

- They must feel they know how to help. People don't offer help for lots of reasons associated with self-perceived competence. Perceived ignorance about mechanical issues means people may not help a stranded motorist.

- They must decide to help. People don't assist others for various reasons. They may be embarrassed by memories of volunteering to help and being rebuffed because of a misinterpretation of the situation. In litigious societies they may be worried about legal implications of helping in certain situations (young children, torn clothes) or simply that the cost to themselves (in terms of time, possibly money) is too high.

the condensed idea
Is there such a thing as altruism?

27 Cognitive dissonance

Most of us feel the need to justify our actions however odd and bizarre they may be. People who smoke know that nicotine addiction is seriously harmful to health. But they are often past-masters at self-justification. They say things like 'smoking is not nearly as dangerous as people say', or 'I had an uncle who smoked 60 a day for 70 years and died happily at 90'.

The theory Cognitive dissonance theory asserts that when we behave inconsistently with our beliefs and attitudes, we experience a negative state called cognitive dissonance which we try to resolve by changing our attitudes or behaviour (or both) to reduce the inconsistency. That is, our attitudes change because we are strongly motivated to maintain consistency in our beliefs and thoughts (cognitions). We are powerfully motivated to achieve consonance. So, behaviour change can lead to attitude change more easily than the other way around.

> **'If the art of magic is essentially producing dissonance, and if human nature abhors dissonance, why is the art of magic still flourishing?'**
> **R.B. Zajonc, 1960**

Cognitive dissonance celebrates the 'insufficient justification effect': when our actions are not fully explained by external rewards (like money) or coercion (like orders) we will experience dissonance, which we can reduce by justifying what we have done.

Conditions Dissonance is aroused and has to be reduced under very specific situations. Just noticing that our behaviour is inconsistent with our attitudes is insufficient. Firstly, people must feel that their attitude is freely chosen, completely voluntary and

timeline

1930s	1946
Writings on the 'consistency principle'	Heider's balance theory

> **The "cognitive dissonance" hypothesis ... would appear to be based upon a culture-specific discomfort Americans have with noticing themselves being inconsistent from one occasion to another or possessing mutually inconsistent aims.**
>
> **N. Much, 1995**

that they are personally responsible for it. If they act under coercion from some external force or threat (or lack of choice), dissonance is not necessarily aroused. One study tested this by either asking or ordering students to write an essay on a controversial topic they did not personally support. The most dramatic shift in their beliefs occurred in those who chose to write the essays.

Secondly, individuals must feel that this attitude-discrepant behaviour is firmly committed and irrevocable. If the behaviour is easily modifiable, this reduces dissonance. In one study people were told they either could or could not meet a person (victim) they had been publicly negative about. Those who believed they could apologize felt less dissonance than those who could not take back what they said.

Thirdly, they must believe that their behaviour has important consequences for themselves and others. If the consequences are minor or trivial they are unlikely to experience any dissonance. Finally, people experience most dramatic dissonance pressure when the particular attitudes or behaviour concerned are central to their self-concept, self-worth and values.

In another study students were asked to write essays that expressed opinions quite different from their own. Some had the essays ignored or even ripped up while others were told they would be used in advertising or on the web. Those who had their counter-attitudinal views potentially exposed were most motivated to shift their attitudes to resolve their dissonance.

The paradoxes of dissonance
The theory states the following:

- if a person is forced to behave in ways contrary to their belief, they will experience dissonance

1957	1960s	1980s
Festinger's cognitive dissonance described	First post-decisional dissonance studies conducted	Theory used extensively in 'persuasive communications'

- the greater the force compelling the behaviour, the less the dissonance and vice versa
- dissonance can be reduced by changing attitudes
- attitude change is greatest when forces to act are paradoxically minimal.

This was illustrated in a famous study conducted in 1959. Three groups of students were required to perform a long, dull, repetitive and monotonous task. Some were paid one dollar, some 20 dollars and the control group nothing. Afterwards they were asked about the task. Those paid only $1 had persuaded themselves the task was more enjoyable and interesting than those paid $20. The $1 people have a dilemma: could/should they admit that they had been 'bought' for a 'paltry sum', a cheap bribe? Not easily. So they re-interpreted the event. The $20 person had less of a problem: people do lots of things if the money is right.

We like to think of ourselves as decent, kind, moral individuals who are just and unlikely to cause innocent people harm or distress. So if we do something hurtful, like shout at, ignore or even hit another person, our dissonance is aroused. If we can't 'take back' this behaviour by apology or compensation, the easiest way to resolve our dilemma is to derogate the victim further by pointing out how bad they were, fully deserving of our ill-treatment to them.

Initiation rites

Cognitive dissonance theory also predicts why people come to like and approve of what they have suffered for. Thus those who perhaps experience corporal punishment (beating or caning at school) claim it did them good, not harm, and that others would benefit from it. Similarly, those who undergo painful or humiliating initiation rites to groups or societies tend later to value and support the experience. Dissonance theory suggests that we justify our painful experiences by upgrading the status of the group that caused us pain. This is sometimes called the severity of initiation test.

In one study, women were asked to judge how interesting they found a rather dull and pointless group discussion about sex. To do the task they had to be screened. One group had simply to read a list of words with mildly sexual meanings (e.g. 'prostitute') while others had to read obscenities and passages from explicitly erotic novels. The aim was to make the screening either highly embarrassing or not. The prediction, which was confirmed, was that the embarrassed group would justify their 'screening test' but rated the discussion as much more interesting than the non-embarrassed group.

Dissonance, selling and persuasion Salespeople know that consistency is valued by society: inconsistency may be thought of as hypocrisy or dishonesty. Consistency also makes us more efficient because we don't have to go through a new decision process each time we confront a new situation.

The idea is that once we make a choice or take a stand/give a commitment, we will encounter personal and interpersonal pressure to behave consistently with that commitment. That is why salespeople ask such questions as 'would you buy if the price was right?' Their idea is to get you committed to a position, possibly quickly, even unthinkingly, which you feel you should honour.

Thus 'compliance professionals', be they doctors, salesmen or teachers, try to induce people to make a verbal commitment that is consistent with the behaviour they will at a later stage request from people. These commitments work best when they are done publicly, take some effort and appear completely voluntary. Often people add new justifications to support the wisdom of their early decisions. Thus our drive to look and be consistent is a powerful weapon on the sales armoury, often causing us to act in ways that are not in our own best interest.

Dissonance after decisions

Many of the important decisions we make, like accepting a job or buying a house, involve making difficult choices. Many people draw up lists of pluses and minuses to help them make a well-informed choice. In this sense people are painfully aware of their cognitive dissonance.

Study after study have shown that we justify our decisions after having made them by upgrading the decision we have made and downgrading the decision we turned down. It has been called 'buyer's nostalgia'. People notice that they read advertisements for the products they have bought more often, enthusiastically and closely after (not before) they made the purchase. After decisions the grass grows less green on the other side of the fence.

Thus studies have shown that gamblers say they feel more confident about winning after they have placed their bet than beforehand. Voters feel more positive towards the candidate they voted for than before actually voting.

the condensed idea
Avoiding inconsistency is a powerful motivation

28 Gambler's fallacy

Dear Abby: **My husband and I just had our eighth child. Another girl, and I am one really disappointed woman. I suppose I should thank God that she was healthy, but, Abby, this one was supposed to have been a boy. Even the doctor told me the law of averages was in our favour 100 to one.[1]**

[1] From the *Dear Abby* column by Abigail Van Buren, United Press Syndicate.

From the Roman philosopher, Cicero, through the Renaissance and right up to the present day, priests, mathematicians and scientists have devoted themselves to uncovering the laws of probability. Yet, for many people, the whole business of chance, risk and odds remains mysteriously opaque. Consider, for example, the doctor who told Dear Abby's 'disappointed woman' that the odds of her having a boy were 100 to 1. In fact, before she gave birth, there were only two possible outcomes – a girl or a boy. Thus, the odds of her giving birth to a boy were not 100 to 1 but 1 to 1. How did her doctor get it so wrong? The answer to this deceptively simple question tells us a great deal about how people think.

'**Probability is the very guide of life.**'

Cicero, 100 BC

The city built on a fallacy The doctor believed that his patient's chances of having a boy were high because she had given birth to seven girls in a row. Roulette players who bet on red because the last seven numbers to come up were black are using the same logic. The problem is that a roulette wheel has no memory; each spin is independent of the last one. The probability of red is exactly the same no matter how many times black has come up. Similarly, the probability of having a baby boy has

timeline

nothing to do with earlier births. The failure to recognise this is known as the *gambler's fallacy*. It is also known as the *Monte Carlo fallacy*, probably because it is largely responsible for the casino city's profitable existence. The gambler's fallacy is important to psychologists because it provides a window into how people make complex judgments.

Representativeness heuristic Many judgement tasks make cognitive demands that are beyond our information processing capacity. When this happens, we cope by relying on strategies known as *heuristics* – mental shortcuts that allow us to make judgements quickly and efficiently. These rules-of-thumb are similar to intuitions; they allow us to function without constantly stopping to think through problems from first principles. The problem is that, while heuristics are often helpful, they can also lead to errors. An example is the *representativeness* heuristic, which, in its simplest form, states that we should judge the probability of an event by how well it 'represents' our experience. For example, the sun always rises in the east, so we are probably correct to assume that it always will. It never rises in the west, so it is a good guess that it never will. The representativeness heuristic usually leads to good judgements, but not always. Consider, for example, the following problem:

> ❛**The mind has its illusions as the sense of sight.**❜
> **Pierre Simon Laplace, 1825**

All families of six children in a city were surveyed. In 72 families the exact order of births of boys and girls was GBGBBG (B=boy, G=girl). What is your estimate of the number of families surveyed in which the exact order of births was BGBBBB?

As each birth is an independent event, these two birth orders are equally likely (as are all other birth orders). Yet, when Nobel Laureate Daniel Kahneman, and his associate, Amos Tversky, put this question to a group of university educated people, more than 80% believed that the second birth order was only half as likely as the first. Their reasoning went like this: the first sequence has 3 girls and 3 boys; a ratio that represents the general population better than the 5 to 1 ratio of the second birth order. Since the

1770
P. Simon Laplace: fallacies
are cognitive delusions

1957
H. Simon: judgements exceed
cognitive capacity

1972
Kahneman and Tversky:
judgement heuristics

first birth order is more 'representative', it is judged more likely. To the 'disappointed woman's' doctor, seven girls in a row was not representative of the 50:50 distribution of boys and girls in the population, so he predicted that the next baby would even things up by being born a boy.

More than gambling Representativeness is such a compelling heuristic; it can even cause health panics. For example, from time to time someone observes that particular workplaces, schools or hospitals have suffered a larger than 'normal' number of cancers. These are known as cancer clusters. The usual response is to look for an environmental cause: high tension wires, for example, or air quality or the emanations of mobile phone towers. Public pressure causes health authorities to dedicate their scarce resources to tracking down the cause. But they rarely find one because the observation was flawed in the first place. Expecting every building and every workplace to have the same distribution of cancer cases as the general population is the same as expecting every family to have an equal number of boys and girls or every run of the roulette wheel to have the same number of red and black outcomes. Random events can, and do, produce clusters; failing to understand this produces unnecessary panic and wastes precious resources that would be better used to solve real problems rather than imaginary ones.

Understanding risk Behavioural economists have shown how poor people are at thinking statistically. They have a sort of numbers numbness. Consider this example:

> 'Fred is described by those who know him as a quiet, studious, introvert. He is detail-oriented, not very assertive and not particularly sociable.'

How to win big at Lotto

Here's a way to make your knowledge of psychology pay off. If you play the National Lottery's Lotto game, and you want to maximise your winnings, choose six sequential numbers (1, 2, 3, 4, 5, 6 or 22, 23, 24, 25, 26, 27 or some other orderly pattern). Because they do not 'represent' what most people think of as a realistic outcome, few people choose these number sequences. Because all sequences have the same chance of winning (practically none), you are no more or less likely to win by choosing six sequential numbers. But, if, by chance, your numbers do come up, at least you won't have to share your prize with anyone.

Do you think he is more likely to be a librarian or a salesman? How much would you bet on your answer? A 'no-brainer': the stereotypical librarian. But wait: how many librarians are there in this country and how many people are in sales? There are probably 100 times as many people in sales than there are in libraries. And they differ between themselves massively depending on what they are selling. Fred might be selling very specialised, highly technical equipment to research scientists. This issue is called 'ignoring the base rate': knowing the overall odds in any situation.

Know your odds What are the odds of winning the lottery? Lower than being struck by lightning, bitten by a poisonous snake or having a crash in an aeroplane. People remain frightened of sharks in waters where they are never seen because of the film *Jaws* that came out over 30 years ago. The same is true of buying insurance policies. Should you insure yourself against plane crashes or being burgled? The latter, of course, because it is more common: the former (thankfully) is very rare.

Apart from the base-rate issue there is also the famous 'bigness bias' which leads to statistical errors. People pay more attention to big numbers than they do to small numbers. Number numbness can often best be seen in the way people think about and use their own money. Gary Belsky and Thomas Gilovich – who wrote a book in 1999 about behavioural economics entitled *Why Smart People Make Big Money Mistakes* – suggested some useful tips to overcome poor statistical reasoning:

1. Don't be impressed by short term success: look always at the long term trends.

2. Play averages because chance plays a great role in investments and it's easy to be seduced by short-term chance factors.

3. Know when time is on your side: start early, don't discount the power of inflation.

4. Beware of and know base rates.

5. Always read the fine print because what the large print giveth, the small print taketh away.

the condensed idea
Our cognitive errors provide a window into our minds

29 Judgement and problem-solving

'He is a good judge of people.' 'Personally, I would not trust her judgement.' 'I think they nearly always produce more problems than they solve.' 'We need to form a committee given the importance of this decision.' Problem-solving is at the very heart of the psychology of thinking. It is about different related issues.

Problem-solving is a purposeful, goal-directed, intellectual activity. Some 'problems' are solved pretty quickly, almost automatically, because they are encountered all the time. But there are problems which require restructuring, insight and recalculation. We know from the gestalt psychologists that sometimes prior experience can disrupt and worsen good problem-solving when well-learned responses to particular problems no longer apply because the problem has changed.

> **'Irrationally held truths may be more harmful than reasoned errors.'**
>
> T.H. Huxley, 1960

Heuristics The word 'heuristic' means to discover. It is used in psychology to describe a method (often a short-cut) that people use to try to solve problems. Heuristics are 'rules of thumb'. They are sometimes constructed with algorithms, which are complicated, logical, procedurally driven ways to solve problems.

In everyday decision-making people call on a wide range of simple heuristics that are mostly accurate and effective. They are very useful when trying to make quick decisions and usually employed when it is not easy to get further information. Indeed, one may use many heuristics at the same time to solve a problem.

timeline

We use heuristics to make decisions when we are uncertain, as we are 'cognitive misers'. Heuristics are simple, efficient rules, hard-wired by evolutionary processes or learned. They have been proposed to explain how people make decisions, come to judgements and solve problems, typically when facing complex problems or incomplete information. Consider these examples.

The *representativeness* heuristic This is the assumption that typical (or representative) members of a group or category are encountered most frequently. This tends to ignore base-rate information or the general occurrence of the problem or group in the population. Studies show that people believe that results taken from small samples are as valid as those from larger ones (see Chapter 8).

The *availability* heuristic This is about the ease of bringing to mind instances or occurrences and the effect that has on judgement. Easy-to-recall, vivid, very imaginable instances count disproportionately more than they should. People remember events or concrete examples more vividly and so overemphasize their importance or probability of happening again over other less memorable events. Another example is that people think they are more likely to die in a plane crash than a car crash as incidents of the former are more widely reported and as such easier to recall.

> ‘**Everyone complains of his memory but nobody of his lack of judgment.**’
>
> Duc François de la Rochefoucauld, **1678**

The *anchoring* heuristic This is a cognitive bias that describes the common human tendency to rely too heavily, or 'anchor,' on one trait or piece of information when making decisions. According to this heuristic, people start with an implicitly suggested reference point (the anchor) and make adjustments to it to reach their estimate. In one study, researchers showed that when asked to guess the percentage of African nations which are members of the United Nations, people who were first asked 'Was it more or less than 45 per cent?' guessed lower values than those who had been asked if it was more or less than 65 per cent. Anchoring and adjustment affect other kinds of estimates, like perceptions of fair prices and good deals.

1972	1982	2002
Groupthink described	Kahneman, Slovic and Tversky, *Judgement under Uncertainty: Heuristics and Biases*	Psychologist Kahneman wins Nobel Prize for Economics

Business biases The application of problem-solving biases or errors in business has become to be known as *behavioural economics*. It focuses on common decision-making attitudes with money-related issues. These include:

- confirmation bias, or only looking for information that confirms or is in favour of your ideas
- optimism bias, which is the belief that you are a better judge than others and that misfortune is more likely to occur to them
- control bias, which is the belief that you can influence the outcome of organizational or national events much more than you can
- overconfidence bias, which is the belief that your predictions and judgements are always the best ones
- mental rigidity, which is either over- or under-reacting to everyday events.

> **'It is the capacity for making mistakes which is the mark of higher stages of intelligence.'**
>
> **H. Price, 1953**

There are many more of these and they make disappointing and depressing reading for those convinced of the cool, brilliant rationality of their judgements.

Brainstorming The work on brainstorming is particularly surprising. It has been suggested that people come up with more and better 'creative' solutions while working in brainstorming groups than they do when alone. The idea is that you follow a process ('more is good', freewheeling is encouraged, no criticism is allowed) and get wonderful results. But the data say otherwise: people working alone seem to do better. Why? Firstly, *evaluation apprehension*, meaning people are self-conscious in groups and can self-censor good ideas because others might disapprove. Secondly, *social loafing* comes into play, where people in groups simply let others do all the work. Thirdly, there is the issue of *production blocking*, meaning that people say they cannot think clearly with all the hubbub going on around them. The jury is back . . . if you add together the results of people working alone on a creative problem, they produce better and more answers than a brain-storming group.

Deciding in groups Do people make better judgements in groups or alone? There is some fascinating and rather counterintuitive social psychological literature on this topic. The idea is that in decision-making we go through various steps: we analyse the situation then decide on objectives; next we decide on how we are going to decide (who, when, how and where) and then search for good alternative solutions. We then evaluate the alternatives, make a choice, evaluate it and learn from the consequences. One central question often overlooked is how we decide – should we do it alone, call in experts, have a committee?

Group polarization There is equally interesting work on group polarization. Most people assume that if decisions are made by a group (such as a board meeting or a criminal jury) they tend to make more moderate and less extreme decisions than individuals making the same judgement alone. However, group decision-making often leads to more extreme decisions. First, many people do social comparisons, that is, comparing themselves with others in the group. In doing so they try more strongly to uphold certain cultural values about fairness, justice, risk, etc. So on issues like environmental pollution or child protection, groups are likely to be very conservative and risk-averse (more than individuals) while on other issues like advising on job changes or adventure holidays they are the reverse. Next, in groups they may hear some very persuasive information given by a confident and articulate person that sways them strongly towards one position.

Groupthink

Many studies on groups who have made very poor decisions have led to the development of the concept of groupthink. This occurs when groups have the illusion that they are invulnerable and where they spend too much time rationalizing (as opposed to being rational about the subject at hand). They tend to believe completely that they are morally and ethically superior to others and indeed spend a lot of time negatively stereotyping others. They also experience strong and unhealthy conformity pressure to 'toe the line' or 'express loyalty'. This leads them to self-censor dissenting ideas and provide good or important counter-arguments. In fact these groups often have 'mind-guards' who ensure that everyone is thinking in the same way. This leads to the impression of unanimity where none really exists.

the condensed idea
Judgement is often influenced by context

30 Too much invested to quit

Your favourite artist is in a show and you have tickets. On the day of the show you learn two heart-sinking things: your star is unwell and will be replaced by an understudy, and also there is a transport strike, making getting to and from the event a nightmare. What if your tickets were a gift from a grateful client or friend? What if you personally paid £100 each?

The *sunk-cost fallacy* shows very clearly that people would more likely struggle along to get to a concert to see someone they did not even know if they themselves had paid for the tickets. Conference organizers say the same thing: people are much more likely to pitch up (and therefore not cancel) the more they pay. This is classic *loss aversion*. An unused ticket means a loss; worse than that, you are being wasteful.

On the way home from work you see an excellent bargain: a really good ready meal at 25 per cent of the usual cost. You snap up one but when you get home you feel like having a friend around. You phone, she agrees, so you pop out for another bargain. But – damn your luck – they ran out of the special offers so you have to buy another of the meals at full price. Worse is to come: you heat up both meals and then your friend phones to say something has come up and she can't make it. You have two hot, unreheatable meals: you have to throw one away. Despite the fact that the meals are identical, people nearly always eat the one for which they paid full price.

'It is better to have loved and lost than never to have loved at all.'

Alfred Lord Tennyson, 1880

timeline

1968	1979
First classic experiment	Prospect theory discussed

Economic thinking Economists argue that sunk costs are not taken into account when making rational decisions. Here is a classic example. You make a mistake in buying a movie ticket which is non-refundable. It is a sunk cost. You can choose between the following two options:

- having paid the price of the ticket, watching the movie that you don't want to see
- having paid the price of the ticket, you say 'too bad' and use the time to do something more fun.

So you regret buying the ticket, but your current decision should be based on whether you want to see the movie at all, regardless of the price, just as if you were to go to a free movie. The rational thinker will probably suggest that since the second option involves suffering in only one way (you spent/wasted the money), while the first involves suffering in two (wasted money *and* time), the second option is obviously preferable.

> **The past is a foreign country. They do things differently there.**
> L. Hartley, 1950

Many people hate 'wasting' resources. Many would feel obligated to go to the movie despite not really wanting to, because doing otherwise would be wasting the ticket price: hard-earned, post-tax money poured away. This is the sunk-cost fallacy: note 'fallacy'. Strictly this behaviour is irrational: it is inefficient because it misallocates resources (time) by depending on information that is irrelevant to the decision being made.

Sunk costs often cause costs to overrun alarmingly. An example of sunk costs may be investment in a factory, machinery or research project that turns out to have a lower value than expected or, worse, no value whatsoever. A government may have spent £50 million on building a really necessary nuclear power plant but the money runs out. The present value is almost zero because it is incomplete.. However, it can be completed for an additional £20 million, or completely abandoned and a different green windpower facility built for a mere £10 million. The abandonment and construction of the alternative facility is the more rational decision, even though it represents a total loss on the original expenditure. The £50 million invested is a sunk cost.

> **Dreams are always set in the past.**
> A. Phillips, 1993

1985	1999	2000
Major paper on the topic	Belsky and Gilovich give help to loss avoiders	Cohen, *The Psychology of the Stock Market*

But how often would politicians be (economically) irrational and choose completion of the project?

Psychologists recognize that sunk costs often affect decisions due to loss aversion: the price paid in the past becomes a benchmark for the value at present and in the future, whereas the price paid should be and is irrelevant. This is therefore non-rational behaviour. People are trapped by their past; they try to make up for bad decisions, to recoup losses.

Classic study

In 1968, in what is perhaps the classic sunk-cost experiment, two researchers approached 141 horse gamblers: 72 of the people had just finished placing a $2.00 bet within the past 30 seconds, and 69 people were about to place a $2.00 bet in the next 30 seconds. Their hypothesis was that people who had just committed themselves to a course of action (betting $2.00) would reduce post-decisional dissonance by believing more strongly than ever that they had picked a winner. They asked the gamblers to rate their horse's chances of winning on a seven-point scale. People who were about to place a bet rated the chance that their horse would win at an average of 3.48, which corresponded to a 'fair chance of winning', whereas people who had just finished betting gave an average rating of 4.81, which corresponded to a 'good chance of winning'. Their hypothesis was confirmed – after making a $2.00 commitment, people became more confident their bet would pay off. They performed an ancillary test on the patrons of the horses themselves and managed (after normalization) to repeat their finding almost identically.

The sunk-cost fallacy is also sometimes known in Europe as the 'Concorde effect'. The British and French governments in the 1950s and 1960s both continued to fund the joint development of the fantastic supersonic Concorde aeroplane even after it became apparent that there was no longer an economic case for the aircraft. It always lost money. Privately the British government knew it was a 'commercial disaster' which should never have been started. But this is more about losing face and political imperatives than simply bad decision-making.

Throwing good money after bad Behavioural economists have recognized the characteristics of those prone to loss aversion and the sunk-cost fallacy. They say classic signs are if you make important spending decisions on how much you have already spent on a project. They note that loss aversion is associated with a tendency to sell winning investments more readily than losing ones and to take money out of the stock market when prices fall. They make the following suggestions to help one make better decisions.

- Evaluate your tolerance for risk, that is, test your threshold for loss and panicking when things go wrong so that at least you can become more self-aware.

- Diversify, so that if something goes wrong with one aspect of your business/investments/work you will react with less emotionality and more sense.

- Focus on the whole, broad, big picture, looking at long-term goals and strategies so that you are less likely to overreact impulsively when things go wrong.

- Forget the past: it's water under the bridge; don't be a victim of misfortune or bad mistakes. Remember it's not about justifying the past. Look at the current and future situation, not the past.

❛Who controls the past controls the future.❜

George Orwell, 1948

- Try to reframe your losses as gains. A loss may teach valuable lessons; it may decrease a tax burden. You cannot change the past but you can think about it differently.

- Spread your gains and integrate your losses. Try to ensure that positive results come at different times but that bad news comes at once, so you can deal with it and get it out of the way.

- Lighten up and pay less attention to your investments. Don't read about your shares every day but rather once a week. Don't let your natural loss aversion threaten your peace of mind.

the condensed idea
Sunk costs affect decision making

31 Rational decision-making

'Why does man regret, even though he may endeavour to banish any such regret, that he has followed the one natural impulse, rather than the other; and why does he further feel that he ought to regret his conduct. Man in this respect differs profoundly from the lower animals.' C. Darwin, 1862

Problem-solving is similar to, but not the same as, decision-making. In problem-solving you try to come up with good alternative solutions: in decision-making you choose between them. People tend to have habitual ways they make decisions. Perhaps they list pluses and minuses. Perhaps they consult others. Decisions can be made alone or with others; coolly or with a great deal of emotionality.

❝No life is without its regrets or without its consolations.❞

A. Bennett, 1995

Most of us like to believe that most of the time we make rational decisions. In economic jargon this is called utility maximization. We work out what is most likely to occur (probabilistically) and the value (utility) of that outcome to us. We then multiply the two and choose the best. This is called normative theory. But there is one central problem: studies of people making decisions show they don't do it like this, particularly when it comes to gains and losses. We attach more to the possibility of loss than gain.

Prospect theory Kahneman and Tversky won the 2002 Nobel Prize in Economics for their work on prospect theory, which describes decisions between alternatives that involve risk, i.e. alternatives with uncertain outcomes, where the probabilities are known.

timeline

1947
Normative theories of decision-making

1981
The importance of framing described

Studies have shown that individuals are much more sensitive to loss than to gain – so much so that they are often willing to get involved in serious risk-taking to avoid losses. It means people sell shares (unwisely) when the stock market dips; they repair an old, failing car again and again because they have already paid for many repairs.

People decide which outcomes they see as basically identical and they set a reference point and consider lower outcomes as losses and larger as gains. The asymmetry of the S-curve is indicative of Warren Buffett's finding that 'losses gain twice the emotional response of gains'. People are risk-averse (play it safe) in relation to gains, yet loss-averse (gamble to avoid losses). The subjective value of a large gain is not much greater than that of a small gain, so there is little incentive for people to gamble in order to try to increase the size of the gain.

The S-curve

An important implication of prospect theory is the framing of risky situations. The following example highlights just what an effect framing has on people.

People were asked to imagine being a scientist working on an outbreak of an unusual disease, which is expected to kill 600 people. Two different programmes to combat the disease have been proposed. The first group of participants were presented with a choice between two programmes:

Programme A: 200 people will be saved.

Programme B: There is a one-third probability that 600 people will be saved, and a two-thirds probability that no people will be saved.

In this group, 72 per cent of participants preferred programme A while the remainder, 28 per cent, opted for programme B.

The second group were presented with the choice between:

Programme C: 400 people will die.

Programme D: There is a one-third probability that nobody will die, and a two-thirds probability that 600 people will die.

‘While the doctor is reflecting, the patient dies.’

Italian proverb

> **There is no more miserable human being than one in whom nothing is habitual but indecision.**
>
> W. James, 1890

In this decision frame, 78 per cent preferred programme D, with the remaining 22 per cent opting for programme C. However, programmes A and C, and programmes B and D, are effectively identical. A change in the decision frame between the two groups of participants produced a preference reversal, with the first group preferring programme A/C and the second group preferring B/D.

Framing effects How you present, dress-up or frame a situation has a powerful impact on how people respond. Would you rather get a 5 per cent discount, or avoid a 5 per cent surcharge? The same change in price framed differently significantly affects consumer behaviours and is an area of huge importance to marketing. Hence the following typical advertisement: 'If you don't sign up by the 15th you may well lose . . .'

When choices involve possible gains people tend to avoid risks, but when choices involve possible losses they will take risks in order to minimize those losses. People of all backgrounds and ages would rather minimize the displeasure of loss than maximize the pleasure of gain.

In one study, two health videos were made to try to persuade women to undertake both a breast examination and a mammogram. Both were nearly identical and presented the same medical and statistical facts. But one emphasized the gains of having the scan, the other the risks in not having it. As the theory predicted, more women who had watched the risk-focused film chose to have a scan.

Studies show that if you want people to indulge in healthy preventative behaviour (like using contraceptives and condoms), the best messages highlight the benefits of using them. However, if you want to get people to take up detection medicine (HIV tests), then focusing on the negative works best. Whether one sees the behaviours as low risk or high risk dictates whether a loss- or gain-framed message works best.

It is not the reality of the loss that matters but the perception of that loss. Once we have committed a lot of time, money and/or energy to any cause, it is extremely difficult to convince us that it was not a good idea or worth support.

Entrepreneurial risk-taking Is risk-taking essentially a personality factor? There are clearly risk-averse and risk-taking individuals. Is it that risk-averse people are very concerned with security, while

Decision paralysis

Prospect theory explains both why we act when we shouldn't, and why we don't act when we should. Curiously, the more choices that people have in life, the more likely they are to do nothing, and the more attractive options there are, the worse the delay or paralysis. The freedom to choose can cause serious problems. The longer you defer making a decision, the less likely you are to get over the hesitation. One study asked people to complete a questionnaire for a decent reward: some were told the deadline was 5 days, others 21 days and a third group had no deadline. Results: 66 per cent returned in the 5-day deadline, 40 per cent in the 21-day dealine and 25 per cent with the non-time limit.

People with decision paralysis are given the following advice.

- Recognize that not to decide is itself a decision. Postponement, passive-aggressiveness and procrastination are not a good way to show some sort of confidence in the *status quo*.

- Never underestimate opportunity costs. That is, the cost of doing nothing may be higher than the cost of doing something that is 'suboptimal'.

- Have an auto-pilot system that requires you to follow certain rules and don't get hung up with making too many decisions.

- Don't forget to play devil's advocate: challenge assumptions, start from scratch, not where you are today. Turn the problem upside-down.

risk-takers, indeed risk-seekers, are motivated by a desire to gain? Risk-seekers show their mettle when there are possible losses, while risk-avoiders do so when there is potential for gain.

Studies of successful entrepreneurs show that they are certainly not risk-averse. They tend to be very active and curious and be willing to take 'moderate' risks. They are energetic and achievement-oriented and optimists. They are prepared to accept failure and learn from mistakes. They seek out opportunities. So in prospect-theory terms they have low loss and risk aversion and are risk-seeking. They tend to reframe decisions so they are positive and are rarely paralysed by indecision.

the condensed idea
Reason has a role
in risk-taking

32 Remembrance of things past

'The reminiscence comes of sunless dry geranium, and dust in crevices, smells of chestnuts in the streets, and female smells in sheltered rooms, and cigarettes in corridors and cocktail smells in bars.' T.S. Eliot, 1945

Nearly everyone will say that certain songs, scents or tastes 'bring it all back'. A distinctive smell can elicit immediate and powerful memories. The songs of one's adolescence can immediately transport one back to a time and a series of feelings long forgotten. And to taste the food of one's childhood or homeland can cause people to have sudden and sometimes quite unexpected memories.

People in marketing know this well. They pump in smells to shops to emphasize a season of the year (pine cones at Christmas, coconut oil for

Forgetting

Many older people can remember things much more clearly about their secondary school days than what happened last year. Interestingly, our ability to recognize faces seems to last much longer than our ability to put a name to them.

If you are taught a language at school or university you forget a great deal in the ensuing two to four years, but that which is retained seems to be quite robust after that, staying much the same for 40 years or more. Once you learn how to swim, drive or skate, this skill seems to be easily retained – that is, if the skill involves what is called closed loops, where one action leads clearly on to the next. It is not true in open-looped skills like typing where the actions are unconnected.

timeline

1880s	1913–27
Galton looks at autobiographical memory	Proust, *In Search of Lost Time*

summer) or of a quality (like cleanliness or warmth) that they believe will change a shopper's mood and hence willingness to buy. They play mood music to try to have the same effect.

Autobiographical memory

We all have memories about the past: childhood, schooling, adolescence, a first job. We have memories of very specific events and of more general events. We may have memories about very specific facts (the weather on our wedding day; the make of our first car) which are verifiable. Looking back, people have strongest memories about two phases of their life: their adolescence and early adulthood (say 12–25) and the last half-dozen years.

Most of us have *infantile amnesia*: we remember little about our early years. Different explanations have been put forward to account for this. It could be that the brain is underdeveloped and so can't store the information, or else we don't have enough sophisticated language to store memories. Maybe the child's view of the world is so different from that of the adult that while memories do remain, we have no real way of accessing them.

One way of studying the phenomenon is to question children and their mothers about the details, say, of the birth of a sibling. They may be asked when or whether the mother went to hospital, who was the replacement carer; the number and type of visits made, etc. Studies using this technique found that children remember around two-thirds as much as their mother, but before the age of three almost nothing at all.

A central question is which 'facts' we remember and which we forget and whether this is systematically distorted. Certainly our ability to recall the past may be influenced by different things, like whether people kept a diary or whether audio and/or film recordings were made of various events. Memories are distorted, constructed and reconstructed over time, particularly if events are frequently or very rarely retold. People interpret the meaning or significance of events rather than the details. Equally they may have one or two very strong images (pictures, sounds) which are integrated into a whole. There is all the difference between an autobiographical fact and a generic personal memory.

> **Much of what is remembered is reconstructed from stored fragments.**
> J. Fodor, 1975

Methods It was the great British psychologist Sir Francis Galton who first started looking at personal recollections in the 1880s. He did so by giving people a single word like 'house' or 'father' and asking them to recollect some specific event associated with that noun. The detail, tone and vividness were all rated by Galton. Other researchers have developed an interview schedule to try to map an individual's recollections of people and events and understand the process by which they occur. The real issue for the progress of scientific study is verifying these actual memories.

> **Our memories are card indexes consulted and then returned in disorder by authorities whom we do not control.**
>
> **Cyril Connolly, 1950**

There is also the fascinating record of a Dutch psychologist who studied his own autobiographical memory for over six years. Every day he recorded a few events that happened to him, over 2,400 in all. Then he tested his memory for them every 12 months, seeing if he could answer who, what, where and when questions. He found the 'when' questions most difficult to answer. He also found, perhaps unsurprisingly, that the more unusual the event and the more emotionally involving it was, the better the memory was. Interestingly, the more unpleasant the memory, the quicker it seemed to be forgotten. Some things seemed completely forgotten but with enough prompts or cues almost everything was recalled.

Studies have shown that how memories are probed affects their recall. Being asked to recognize rather than recall things has a great impact, with the former being much better than the latter. Also much depends on whether events were formally recorded in a diary (even a video diary).

Distorting, clouding and confabulating One important distinction made is that between *truth* and *accuracy*. If a person recalls the gist of a situation (general experience and feelings), it could be described as true; but it is only accurate if it is correct in every detail. In this sense most autobiographical memory is true. Most ordinary people have autobiographical recollections that are relatively error-free in the sense that they remember the broad outline of their lives correctly, but if asked to give detailed information they make mistakes.

Some people, usually those with amnesia caused by brain damage, have clouded memories. This means they seem at different times to remember things but at other times they are lost. Thus they seem to have their information stored but it is difficult at times to access. Still other brain-damaged patients have been known to give highly detailed but obviously wrong autobiographical accounts of events. Some seem unable to distinguish between genuine and made-up memories and have what are called 'dysexecutive' problems. This is very rare, however.

Flashbulb memories

This is a term for highly memorable, often very specific personal memories about a major event. The term was introduced in 1977 when researching memory for the assassination of John Kennedy in 1963. There are six factors associated with flashbulb memories:

- place, or where the event occurred

- ongoing event, or what you were doing at the time

- nature of the informant, that is, how you found out

- the effect on other people

- your own emotional reaction

- the immediate aftermath to this event.

Some autobiographical memories are like this but they normally refer to famous historical events.

Biodata Many people assert that the past predicts the present: that your personal history explains in large part the sort of person that you are. Hence the fascination with biographies. Clinical, but also business, psychologists have been interested in this phenomenon in trying to predict how well people will perform in specific jobs – taking into account how many different schools you went to; whether you are a first-born child; if you were elected a prefect at school; the age at which you got married and so on. Typically the data are about a person's educational, work and personal history including facts about health, relationships, hobbies, money and personal habits. This selection method attempts to ensure that only biographical facts are admitted as evidence.

the condensed idea
Different stimuli
can trigger memory

33 What the witness saw

Could you accurately identify the person who sold you a newspaper this morning? And what if you were woken by a burglar whom you just saw fleetingly – are you sure you would 'finger' the right person in a classic identity parade? How many people languish in prison because of confident, but wrong, identification just because they looked 'a criminal type'? And how many people get off serious crimes scot-free because they were not identified by one or more witnesses?

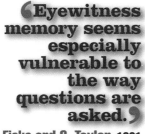

'**Eyewitness memory seems especially vulnerable to the way questions are asked.**
S. Fiske and S. Taylor, 1991

The psychology of eyewitness identification is one of the most important areas of applied psychology at the intersection of psychology and the law. Lawyers, judges, the police and psychologists are very aware of the frequent miscarriage of justice because of wrongful convictions. They know of the power of identification to juries, particularly if the witness seems clear-headed, confident and articulate.

Jurors overestimate the importance of eyewitness reports: conviction rates rise from 20 per cent to 70 per cent with just one witness testimony. Most people are completely unaware of just how many different factors can falsely influence our recollection of events. Poor viewing conditions, brief exposure, and stress, are the more established factors, yet expectations, biases, personal stereotypes, and leading questions can all intervene to create erroneous reports.

timeline

1890	1904
William James talks of imagined memory	Studies begin on event recall

The witness Some factors are to do with the individual witness: their sex, age, race as well as their personality and education; and perhaps more importantly, their training and experience of people and event observation – all could influence accuracy of recall. Women notice different things from men but there is only limited evidence of sex differences in eyewitness accuracy. Older people may have less good sight and memory: we know young adults perform best at this task. We are better at identifying people from our own racial group.

Contextual factors There are a host of situational factors associated with the event that was witnessed. These include the type of crime; the complexity, duration and actual involvement in the event; as well as simple factors like how dark it was, the time of day and the number of others present. The more stressed the eyewitness, the less they recall accurately. Also there is an established 'weapon-focus effect' so that if a gun or knife is involved in an incident it seems to command a lot of attention and correct eyewitness identification declines.

Social factors There are social factors associated with the constraints and regulations of the courtroom and the social status of the interrogator. People's expectations can have very powerful effects. Cultural biases, latent prejudices, political attitudes all have an effect. The language used in court can also have a powerful effect. In a famous study, different words were used about a car crash: 'bump', 'collide', 'contact', 'hit', 'smash'. The words influenced later recall. Thus if the word 'smash' was used, people were more likely to erroneously say they saw broken glass than if the word 'bumped' was used.

> **❝All techniques that claim to provide such memory "playbacks" – the major example is hypnosis – have been found wanting . . . the tape recorder theory is false.❞**
> **Henry Gleitman, 1981**

Interrogational issues There are many important factors associated with the interrogational methods and tools such as ID parades, photofits and artist's sketches. Consider something as simple but important as the 'line-up'. First question: should the suspected culprit be in the line-up or not? We know from evidence that when the actual perpetrator of the crime is not present, the police suspect has a significantly higher chance of being incorrectly identified. If the witness is told the guilty person may or

1976	**1979**	**1988**
British legal committee (Devlin) on eyewitness testimony	Loftus, *Eyewitness Testimony*	The cognitive interview conceived

may not be present, the likelihood of a mistake sharply decreases in comparison with when the witness assumes the guilty person has to be there.

The line-up administrator may easily 'leak' information and influence the witness. Hence it is recommended that it is done by someone not connected to the case. Next, it helps if witnesses are given feedback on their errors if they choose 'known innocents' who have been asked to be in the line-up but could not be identified with the crime. Of course the innocents or 'fillers' should resemble the witness descriptions. If the criminal is remembered as tall, bald, thin and spectacled, then all the fillers should be as well, because we know that anyone with these characteristics (innocent or guilty) is more likely to be fingered. We also know that errors are more likely to occur if people are shown the full line-up simultaneously rather than sequentially.

When people make an eyewitness judgement there is always some element of doubt. However, they tend to express more confidence later than at the time of the judgement, even when it was relatively uncertain. 'Maybe' or 'probably' often turns into 'clearly'. Therefore to reduce error it is advised that the witness's confidence is recorded at exactly the same time they first make their identification.

Experimental work One early experiment showed people a clip of a car crash and then asked them to estimate the speed of the vehicles when they either 'contacted' or 'smashed' into each other. The response was directly related to the force implied by the verb, ranging from 32mph to 41mph. Leading questions have had many replicable findings, with just subtle changes to wording leading to a dramatic effect on testimony; 'did you see a. . .' compared to 'did you see *the*. . .' being just one example of how changing one word can influence respondents.

Most witnesses are obliging as they want to help, and in the case of a violent crime or assault, they have an added incentive to help the police capture a violent criminal. Witnesses believe the police would not conduct a line-up unless they had a good suspect. Although witnesses try hard to identify the true criminal, when they are uncertain – or when no one person in the line-up exactly matches their memory – they will often identify the person who best matches their recollection of the criminal. And often their choice is wrong.

Jurors may be unaware of the factors that can interfere with eyewitness perception, such as the weapon-focus effect, or factors that interfere with memory storage, such as the effect of prior exposures on suspect identification, and this may be why a review of 205 cases of wrongful arrest found that 52 per cent of these cases were associated with mistaken eyewitness testimony.

Factors to consider

Lawyers and jurors are often encouraged to consider a range of issues before giving much attention to an eyewitness testimony.

- Did the witness get a good opportunity to observe the person?

- Was the witness's capacity hindered by alcohol, drugs or injury?

- Do the witness and accused know each other?

- Are they of the same race?

- How long ago did the event happen?

- How was the accused identified (photographs, line-up)?

- How confident was the witness at the initial identification?

It has been established that any testimony given in an assertive and positive matter is considered more accurate and truthful. We know that the longer ago an event, the less we remember. We also know that scenes that are vivid, striking or novel are always better recalled than the mundane. Thus various techniques like the cognitive interview have been formulated to improve eyewitness recall. This encourages various specific acts: recounting the story both forward and backward, and from different points of view; reporting all remembered details, however trivial.

the condensed idea
Eyewitness identification is often wrong

34 Artificial intelligence

'We should not invoke any entities or forces to explain mental phenomena if we can achieve an explanation in terms of a possible electronic computer.' M.G. Kendall, 1950

Fact or fiction? Many people have dreamed about making intelligent machines and some have appeared to have done so: robots that can assemble cars; machines that can play chess that beat grand masters. Many ancient myths contained reference to thinking machines, slave-like automatons or frightening monsters who, once created, become uncontrollable. Futurists throughout the last century have written either about wonderful new worlds where machines take all the drudgery out of work or alternatively take over the world. Today artificial intelligence (AI) is at the heart of everything from robots and medical diagnosis to the development of sophisticated toys.

'A machine cannot think any more than a book can remember.'

L.S. Hearshaw, 1987

Defining AI The modern definition of AI is the study and design of *intelligent agents*, systems that perceive their environment and take actions that maximize their chances of success. The term AI is also used to describe a property of machines or programs: the intelligence that the system demonstrates. Researchers hope machines will exhibit reasoning, knowledge, planning, learning, communication, perception and the ability to move and manipulate objects. *General intelligence* (or 'strong AI') has not yet been achieved and is a long-term goal of AI research.

History AI is barely 60 years old. Brilliant mathematicians and engineers built and programmed early computers which could solve

timeline

1941	1955
First electronic computer	First AI program developed

complex logical problems and even speak. Governments and universities poured money into this research and there were optimistic forecasts in the 1960s of what machines could be programmed to do. However, disappointment and disillusionment followed from the 1980s till 2000. The millennium has seen a great revival, thanks to the massive increase in computer power in addition to attempts to help solve very specific problems.

Methods Some machines have been developed to out-perform humans in specific tasks, a famous example being Deep Blue, which beat the then grand master Garry Kasparov at chess in May 1997. Programs like this are specific to only one field and their knowledge base is created for them by humans.

> The question we wanted to ask is this: "Can a digital computer, as defined, think? That is to say "Is instantiating or implementing the right computer program with the right inputs and outputs sufficient for, or constitutive of, thinking?" And to this question ... the answer is clearly "No".
>
> John Searle, 1984

AI researchers develop a number of tools or methods that are designed to help them achieve their difficult task. These include the search function or how they explore their target. Next they need a logic system. These then develop into probabilistic systems for coming to conclusions. At the heart of the work are systems that help classify information and then systems which control actions once that information has been classified.

Computer programs have been developed to learn from experience. An example of this is Soar ('state, operate and result'), which solves problems by starting with an initial state and applying operators until the result state is achieved. Soar can creatively overcome an impasse and has the ability to learn from experience, storing solutions and using them if a similar problem is encountered in the future. This is important in AI development as it can solve a wide variety of problems more efficiently. But, more importantly, Soar behaves similarly to a problem-solving human. Both learn from experience, solve problems and generate similar-shaped learning curves.

1964
Fuzzy logic idea introduced

1970
Expert systems devised

1997
Deep Blue defeats Gary Kasparov

The ethics of AI

Critics have pointed out that those traditionally most interested in AI have been defence agencies and big businesses, particularly computer companies. Does this mean we need to consider the possible ethics of AI? Certainly there are social consequences of all scientific developments.

Knowledge is power: it is often neutral and can be put to use in different ways. Hence we have nuclear power and nuclear weapons. Both criminals and crime prevention and apprehensive professionals may use exactly the same equipment to acquire and process data.

What should intelligent machines be able to do?

Advocates of strong AI believe that machines must and will be able to outsmart or exceed human abilities to think, solve problems and learn. At the heart of the enterprise initially was the ability of AI researchers to build systems that efficiently, accurately and consistently solved problems. This involved writing algorithms to do things such as break codes or solve puzzles. Hence it looked as though machines could be taught to reason: to be logically deductive. The fact that so many psychological studies have shown that humans are often illogical, irrational and inefficient at solving problems only encouraged AI researchers to show how they could outwit humans. More recently researchers have shown how machines can use even incomplete, irrelevant and distorted information to make decisions.

Planning, storing and learning

AI technology is used to make predictions about the future and hence plan for it. This inevitably involves a planning function. Can we devise intelligent machines that could set or choose goals and targets and then actually achieve them?

AI researchers are concerned with more than just 'thinking' but also with knowledge. A central issue for AI is how machines capture, categorize and access knowledge. Related to this is the concept of learning. Can machines be taught to learn? Can they remember correct and incorrect performances and learn to do more of the former and fewer of the latter? Can they deal with completely new information on the basis of programming they have received?

Machines are also being programmed for sophisticated sensory perception. These can be to see (cameras), listen (microphones) or feel (sound) signals and then recognize real objects. These are now moving from object recognition to the much more exciting world of face and person recognition.

AI research has also progressed in the important and tricky business of natural language processing. Many people have dreamt of a machine that can produce typed script of what they say. Equally there are those who dream of machines that could read books (out loud) or even accurately translate one language to another. Progress has been made on all these fronts.

Creative machines?   Could we design machines that are creative? Creativity usually means producing things that are both novel and useful. Equally controversial is the idea that one might produce socially and emotionally intelligent machines. To fully qualify for this accolade, a machine must be able first to read or detect emotions in another person (or machine) and then react to that person or machine appropriately. An emotionally intelligent, socially skilled machine would need to be more than simply polite but also rewarding and sensitive.

The Turing test   In 1950, English mathematician Alan Turing came up with a very simple criterion: a computer would deserve to be called intelligent if it could deceive a human being into believing it was human. In the early 1960s researchers developed a paranoid computer program called PARRY. The program could be set to either of two modes: weakly or strongly paranoid. The test involved having a group of real, qualified psychiatrists interview the 'patient' by teletype. The study found that none of the interviewers believed they were interviewing a computer. More interestingly, a group of psychiatrists were sent various transcripts of interviews with paranoid patients, some real and some computer generated. It was clear they could not distinguish between the two.

> **The real question is not whether machines think but whether people do.**
> **B.F. Skinner, 1969**

By the criterion of the Turing test we have long had intelligent machines: programmable computers that pass as people. By the 1960s computers could converse – strictly accept and answer questions – about all sorts of issues, including those which may occur in a psychiatric interview. Strictly speaking, they did not listen or talk but if you typed in questions they responded with typed answers. They passed the test if the interlocutor believed themselves to be communicating with a real live person.

the condensed idea
Can machines think like humans?

35 Perchance to dream

Why do we enter a fantasy world several times a night when we sleep? Why do we perceive imaginary events and perform imaginary behaviours and what do they mean? Are they a gateway into our unconscious? Can we really interpret our dreams?

Dreams can be frightening or reassuring. Dreams are fantastic in the sense that impossible, illogical things can and do occur. In dreams you can fly; dead people come to life; inanimate objects speak.

> **The dream is the reflection of the waves of the unconscious life in the floor of the imagination.**
>
> **H. Amiel, 1989**

REM sleep Most of us dream on average one to two hours each night, having a variety of dreams. Most dreams are completely forgotten and some people therefore claim not to dream. Researchers have found that if people are awakened directly after a rapid eye movement (REM) sleep episode, many can recall their dreams fairly accurately. A person awakened during REM sleep will almost always report a dream, often in great detail. These reports indicate that people are conscious during sleep, even though they may not always remember the experience. Brain wave studies show we are very active. Also we know that men are likely to have erections and women greater blood flow to the vagina at this time.

Types of dreams It is said the word 'dream' is derived from the words for 'joy' and 'music'. Many people talk of various different kinds of dreams: of highly lucid but also vague dreams; of nightmares and of lovely dreams.

timeline

AD 50	1899
Numerous mentions in the Bible	Freud, *The Interpretation of Dreams*

Children from 3 to 8 years old often report having nightmares but they seem not to appear in their own dreams much before the ages of 3 or 4 years old. Many report recurrent dreams, some which they fear, others which they long for. Some believe that their dreams are prophetic. Nearly two-thirds of people claim that they have had *déjà-vu* dreams.

Certainly there appear cross-culturally common dreams to all people at all times. The flying dream is common: people report that they can fly like a bird, perhaps by doing a swimmer's breast stroke. Others report the falling dream where they fall out of tall buildings or down dark pits for a very long time. Or they just fall over a lot. Many dream of suddenly being naked and hence very embarrassed in front of others. The chase dream is common: most often you are being chased relentlessly by others, or perhaps you are chasing them. Students will know of the test/exam dream where you have to sit a test and despite revision can't remember anything, or worse, are paralysed and just can't write. The dream of losing your teeth is also surprisingly common.

‘Dreams are meaningful only in the context of the dreamer's life.’

D. Broadribb, 1987

Interpretations Inevitably there are various proposed interpretations of these dreams. Does the teeth dream signal that we are very concerned with our physical attractiveness? Or perhaps it represents a loss of power and ageing, or the concern that you are never heard or being overlooked. Perhaps your teeth represent oral weapons and they are falling out because you have been saying untruths about others. It has even been proposed that it is about money: hoping a magical tooth fairy will appear and give you lots of money.

But how to interpret the naked dream? Is it all about vulnerability and shame? You are hiding some information, concealing a relationship, doing something you should not and you feel guilty. Worse, you are scared of being found out, disgraced and ridiculed. Or it could mean that you are feeling unprepared for some major test or task? One curious feature is that you realize you are naked but no one else seems to be paying attention to that fact. This could indicate that you have worries but that you really feel they are unfounded.

1934	1957	2004
Jung, *Memories, Dreams, Reflections*	REM sleep and dreaming connection	Lohff, *The Dream Directory*

Freudian ideas Sigmund Freud proposed that dreams arise out of our inner conflicts between unconscious desires and prohibitions against acting out these desires, which we learn from society. Thus all dreams represent unfulfilled wishes, the content of which is symbolically disguised. The latent content is transformed into the manifest content (plot), which needs to be explained to supposedly unveil the person's unconscious desires. Dreams are symbolic, or metaphors for our true underlying feelings.

> **'This day's residue is transformed by dream work into a dream and made innocuous by sleep.'**
>
> **Sigmund Freud, 1932**

Dream interpretation was Freud's favourite way to get to understand this conflict and so he would encourage people to talk without restraint about their dreams. In his view, dreams concern one's past and present and they arise from unknown regions within. Every dream at its core is an attempt at wish-fulfilment. Dreams are the 'royal road to the unconscious'. In dreaming various processes occur, like *condensation*, where themes are reduced to single images such as an open door or a deep-flowing river. Analysts are particularly interested in *displacement*, where people, things and certain activities replace each other. Then there is *transformation*, where people are transformed to be bigger or smaller, older or younger, more or less powerful.

Freudian theory leads to various predictions about dreaming being tested. Thus males should have more castration anxiety dreams than females, who

Evolutionary psychology

Evolutionary psychologists have noted that many dreams are about threat and danger and they argue that their function is to represent real, everyday threats so that we can face and rehearse different responses. If this were true, most people should report realistic dreams about present or past environmental threats. However, there appear to be three problems with this explanation. Firstly, many dreams are about positive emotions and events, particularly sexual gratification. Secondly, many dreams seem to involve the 'processing' of information that occurred that day or in the recent past that was not necessarily stressful or threatening. Thirdly, it seems unclear how dreaming actually teaches or encourages better adaptation, which is a core concept in evolutionary psychology.

> **❝I was never able to agree with Freud that the dream is a "façade" behind which its meaning lies hidden – a meaning already known but maliciously so to speak withheld from consciousness.❞**
>
> **Carl Jung, 1963**

would have more penis-envy dreams. Males should have more male strangers in dreams who they fight with (the father in the oedipal stage of development).

Critics point out that if dreams are merely wish-fulfilment, why are so many negative? Next, Freud based his theory on those few dreams (less than 10 per cent) that are remembered and articulated by patients. Third, there is a serious problem of reliability in the interpretation of dreams, as different therapists offer very different interpretations. Fourth, as Jung pointed out, dreams seem to have similar content across time and culture regardless of whether they are deeply repressive or surprisingly liberal.

Physical studies Researchers have proposed an explanation for dreaming that does not involve unconscious conflict or desires. In the REM phase of sleep, a circuit of acetylcholine-secreting neurons in the pons within the brain become active, stimulating rapid eye movements, activation of the cerebral cortex and muscular paralysis, which causes us to see images. The eye movements a person makes during a dream correspond reasonably well with the content of the dream; the eye movements are what one would expect if the events in the dream were really occurring. The images evoked often incorporate memories of episodes that have occurred recently or what the person has been thinking about lately. Presumably the circuits responsible are more excited by their recent use. Patients awaiting major surgery reveal their fears in what they dream about during the two or three nights before the operation. Their fears are rarely expressed directly, being about scalpels or operating rooms. Their reference is indirect, in condensed symbolized form. Dreams often express what is currently most important in a person's life, and not any deep underlying wish-fulfilment concept.

the condensed idea
Do dreams provide insights into our unconscious?

36 Try to forget

'If there is anything that we wish to change in a child, we should first examine it and see whether it is not something that could better be changed in ourselves.' Carl Jung, 1954

The essence of the concept of repression is to push away or turn away something. In psychology it is the idea of the banishing of specific mental contents from consciousness to avoid distressing emotions.

Couch, cinema and courtroom

Repression has been investigated in the consulting room, the laboratory and the courtroom. Some of the most fascinating of all psychological cases essentially involve repression. Thus there are cases of *hysterical amnesia*, which is defined as a fugue state where people have complete memory loss, usually as a consequence of trauma. Another is the equally rare case of *multiple personality*, where people have very different personalities which seem to know nothing about each other. These cases particularly appeal to novelists and film-makers.

Recovered memories There have been many charges of child abuse through 'recovered repressed memories'. Criminals who have committed violent acts seem unable to accurately recall the crime, possibly because they have repressed it. It has been claimed that in therapy adults are able to recover memories of childhood abuse that have been long repressed. Both perpetrator and victim have reason to repress the terrible events but of course this is very difficult to prove. It has also been asserted that memories of the past are very easily distorted by the ways in which they are elicited in therapy as well as courtrooms. Experimental studies

timeline

1894	1915
Freud, *Studies in Hysteria*	Freud, 'Repression'

have shown quite clearly that normal, healthy individuals can be convinced that false, incorrect memories are true. Clinicians admit that it is quite possible for people to develop 'illusory' rather than 'repressed then recovered' memories.

Certainly we know that recovered memories have similar characteristics. Most are memories by women of multiple episodes where a father has indulged in some inappropriate sexual practice before her eighth birthday. These memories are 'recovered' in therapy and a fifth get reported to the police. Interestingly, studies of verified abuse finds the age of abuse is later and very rarely by either fathers or stepfathers.

Freud and repression What we're consciously aware of at any one time represents the tip of an iceberg: most of our thoughts and ideas are totally inaccessible at that moment (pre-conscious) or are totally inaccessible (unconscious). Much of what's unconscious exists through repression, whereby threatening or unpleasant experiences are 'forgotten'. They may become inaccessible, locked away from our conscious awareness. This is a major form of *ego* defence. Freud singled it out as a special cornerstone 'on which the whole structure of psychoanalysis rests'. It is the most essential part.

Repression is the process of pulling thoughts into the unconscious and preventing painful or dangerous thoughts from entering consciousness; seemingly unexplainable naïvety, memory lapse or lack of awareness of one's own situation and condition. The emotion is conscious, but the idea behind it is absent.

The inner wars that we all have, according to Freud, have the same rough outline. The conflict begins when the *id*-derived urges, and various

> **Civilization and higher education have a large influence in the development of repression . . . as a result of which what was formerly felt as agreeable now seems unacceptable and is rejected with all possible psychical force.**
> **Sigmund Freud, 1920**

1957	1961	1900
Multiple personality described	Repressors and sensitizers	Defensive repression coping style

associated memories are pushed into the unconscious. However, these urges refuse to stay down, and they find substitute outlets whose further consequence is a host of additional defences that are erected to reinforce the original repression, hold off the *id*-derived flood and allow the *ego* to maintain its self-regard. Repression is at the heart of the antagonism between the *id* and the *ego*.

Freud developed his ideas when studying hysteria. He believed that repression split consciousness and the *ego* and brought about disassociations in personality. The process of repression prevented the healthy and normal discharge of emotion and excitement. It dammed this up. Also it prevented some ideas from being associated with other ideas so that beliefs were properly integrated with one another. Repression essentially weakened the personality: it was an internal saboteur that caused divisions and rifts. Only later did Freud come to believe that it was a normal, healthy and common defence mechanism.

There are two phases that lead a person to repression. *Primary* repression is the process of determining what is self, what is other; what is good, and what is bad. At the end of this phase, the child can distinguish between desires, fears, self, and others. *Secondary* repression begins once the child realizes that acting on some desires may bring anxiety. This anxiety leads to repression of the desire. The threat of punishment related to this form of anxiety, when internalized, becomes the *superego*, which intercedes against the desires of the *ego* without the need for any identifiable external threat.

It is often claimed that traumatic events are repressed, yet it appears that the trauma more often strengthens memories due to heightened emotional or physical sensations. One problem from an objective research point of view is that a 'memory' must be measured and recorded by a person's actions or conscious expressions, which may be filtered through current thoughts and motivations.

The trait of repression In the early 1960s psychologists talked of people being either repressors or sensitizers. Imagine you had to have a serious operation in a couple of weeks. Some people would try to put it to the back of their mind, filling their time with distracting activities (repressors), while others would talk about it constantly (sensitizers). Both are dealing with their anxiety in different ways and there were questions about which approach was more psychologically healthy and adaptive. This idea was revitalized in the 1990s when researchers identified repressors as a personality trait determined by two factors: anxiety and defensiveness. Repressors are low-anxiety, highly defensive people who seem actively engaged in keeping themselves, rather than other people, convinced that they are not prone to negative emotions. They are interesting and unusual because they always claim to be healthy and adjusted, but if you measure their physiological and behavioural responses to things – particularly negative emotions – they react very strongly. They seem to be either deceiving themselves or trying to manage the impression of being tough, resilient and calm when they are far from it.

Cognitive psychology The proposition of 'motivated forgetting', where the motivation is both unconscious and aversive, has never been demonstrated in controlled research. For the cognitive psychologist, repression is simply forgetting something that is unpleasant. Thus studies have been done where experimenters are nasty (vs nice) to people who are trying to learn things and later it was demonstrated they remembered less when the experience was negative as opposed to positive.

> **The process of repression, which sets in during the fourth year of life or thereabouts is, in wit, temporarily suspended.**
> **Karl Marx, 1920**

Studies show that if people are asked to write about their childhood up to the age of 8, about 50 per cent of people have predominantly positive memories, 30 per cent negative and 20 per cent neutral. But this may not be repression in operation: it could be quite simply that most people do have happy childhoods. Another study showed good evidence of repression: mothers who had just given birth were asked to report the quality and quantity of pain that they had just endured. They were then asked to do this again some months later and they all reported less pain.

Another descriptive theory for repression is that it's just a special case of retrieval failure. Maybe memories are not held back by a censor but are just hard to reach due to a lack of relevant retrieval cues. Anxiety may play a role in this, perhaps blocking refilling or impeding retrieval cues, but it is not the cause. This retrieval-blocking interpretation of repression is part of a more general approach.

the condensed idea
Repression is intentional, but unconscious, forgetting

37 Tip-of-the-tongue phenomenon

You are sitting watching a television quiz show. A question comes up on one of your topics. You know you know the answer but you can't seem to get it. You have the feeling of knowing. You know the answer begins with a 'B' and has three syllables, but can't get it out. You have a retrieval block. One study looked at a person trying to remember the German name Kepler. They knew it was 'foreign' and began with a K so they tried Keller, Kellet, Kendler and Klemperer. They knew that Keller was closest but just couldn't access it.

Remembering is an automatic process; the retrieval of information from memory in response to a stimulus is the specific part of memory that is automatic. What is sometimes effortful is the attempt to come up with the internal thoughts that cause the information to be retrieved. The retrieval of implicit memories is automatic: a certain stimulus will evoke an automatic response. For example, riding a bike, or writing one's name – how do we automatically do these correctly?

TOTs But memory is often flawed; we make mistakes and struggle to retrieve the information we seek. Psychologists ask, why does this happen? And what does it show us about the way our memory works? A major area in this field is the tip-the-tongue phenomenon (TOT), an instance of knowing something that cannot immediately be recalled. TOT is a near-universal experience with memory recollection involving difficulty retrieving a well-known word or familiar name. When experiencing TOT,

timeline

300 BC	1965
Aristotle reports TOTs occur mainly with names	First 'feeling of knowing' study

people feel that the blocked word is on the verge of being recovered. Despite failure in finding the word, they have the feeling that the blocked word is figuratively 'on the tip of the tongue'. Inaccessibility and the sense of imminence are two key features of defining TOT. The active search for stimuli that evokes the appropriate response as exemplified by TOT is called recollection.

Feeling of Knowing

There are sophisticated feeling of knowing (FOK) experiments and theories in psychology. One view called the *internal monitor* is that we have a FOK when we have 'no listing is found for an item that is in the directory'. A central debate is whether the problem occurs because of the way we encode or decode information. That is, does it depend on how and where it is stored rather than how it is retrieved? We also know that people can readily distinguish between a subject state of remembering vs knowing: remembering is conscious recollection while knowing is a feeling of familiarity without being able to recall.

Early studies The phenomenon has been studied extensively since the first empirical study was undertaken in 1966. It has been found that people could recall a good deal about the word on the tip of their tongue and would recognize it immediately it was presented to them. Later researchers found evidence of what has been called the 'ugly sister effect', which is repeatedly coming up with the wrong/different words while searching one's memory for the correct one. Ugly sister words are superficially similar but seem more frequently used than the one which is blocked.

People try all sorts of techniques to 'unblock' themselves, which can be very frustrating. They scan their inner and outer world for the solution. Some go through the alphabet or try to envisage something relevant. Some ask others or search the environment. Sometimes the word just 'pops up' spontaneously and for no apparent reason.

1966	**1984**	**1991**
First TOT study	First 'ugly sister effect' study	First review paper

Curiously, it has been found that giving a person clues or cues sometimes has a negative effect, in that people do less well. When people search their memory, all they seem to recall is the clue which puts them off.

So what have we learnt? Firstly, it is a common if not universal experience. One researcher examined 51 languages and found that 45 of them include expressions using the word 'tongue' to describe the TOT state. Secondly, it occurs fairly often, generally once a week, but this increases with age. Thirdly, it often involves proper names and often we can recall the first letter of the word. We can recall a person's hobbies, occupation and hair colour but just not their name. Fourthly – and thankfully – we the solve the problem around 50 per cent of the time.

Theories One theory proposed as to why it occurs has been that the cause of TOT may be in the sound of a word. Instead of focusing on the importance of semantic information – the meaning of word – it may be that the sound of a word is more important. Words contain several types of information, including:

* semantic information (meaning)
* lexical information (letters)
* phonological information (sound).

These types of information are held in separate parts of memory. They are connected of course, so that when, for example, you read 'Velcro', the letter information triggers the connected sound information and the connected meaning information, telling you how to pronounce the word and what it means. When you try to think of a word, as opposed to being given it, you generally start with the meaning ('that sticky stuff that has fuzz on one side and tiny hooks on the other'). If the connection between that meaning and the sound information is not strong enough, the sound information won't be activated sufficiently to allow you to retrieve all of it.

> **The rhythm of a lost word may be there without a sound to clothe it. Everyone must know the tantalizing effect of the blank rhythm of some forgotten verse, restlessly dancing in one's mind, striving to be filled out with words.**
>
> **William James, 1890**

Other theorists think that TOTs occur because of weak connections between the meaning and the sound of a word. Connections are strengthened when they're used a lot. They are also stronger when they've just been used. It may also be that ageing weakens connections. This may explain why the errant word suddenly pops up. It may be that you have experienced a similar sound to the target word.

The TOT has been studied using three different subdisciplines: psycholinguistics, memory perspectives and metacognition. The first two are consistent with direct access, and focus on TOTs as a temporary breakdown in lexical retrieval. This approach has linked TOTs to other errors in spoken language, such as slips of the tongue and spoonerisms. TOTs are a marker of retrieval processes gone awry. The psycholinguistic approach views TOTs as a window on word retrieval.

The direct-access views of the psycholinguistic and memory perspectives fall into three basic hypotheses. The first is the blocking hypothesis, which states that TOTs occur because people recognize blocking words as incorrect but cannot retrieve the correct but inhibited target. The second is the incomplete activation hypothesis, which suggests that TOTs are caused by a sensitivity to the existence of an unrecalled target in memory, accompanied by the failure to retrieve the target into conscious memory. The third hypothesis is the transmission deficit model, which states that TOTs are brought about when the semantic representation of the word is activated, but there is a failure to prime the complete phonological representation of the target word.

> **The memory is sometimes so retentive, so serviceable, so obedient – at others so bewildered and so weak – and at others again so tyrannic and beyond control.**
>
> **Jane Austen, 1810**

Providing support for the direct-access views are research subjects' recognition of TOT targets and their ability to give partial information of TOT targets. Recognition of the correct target following a TOT experience is much greater than recognition of the correct target when subjects are not experiencing a TOT. Moreover, people can usually recall phonological information related to the TOT targets, such as the first letter of the word, the number of syllables and the syllabic stress.

Metacognitive models focus on the role that monitoring and controlling processes play in cognition. This approach views TOTs as inferences based on non-target information that is accessible to rememberers.

the condensed idea
The mistakes we make reveal how memory works

38 Psychosexual stages

'Freud's concept of sexuality is thoroughly elastic, and so vague that it can be made to include almost anything.'
Carl Jung, 1960

Freud changed the way we think about and talk about ourselves. Many of his basic ideas have been popularized and terms from his theories like 'anal-obsessional', 'phallic symbol' or 'penis envy' have bubbled down into everyday language. Freud was a highly original thinker and, without doubt, one of the greatest thinkers of the 19th and 20th centuries. He developed a highly controversial theory, indeed theories, about personality development, mental health and illness.

Freudian theory – the basics Freudian theories make a number of assumptions.

- Behaviour is a result of battles and compromises among powerful, often unconscious motives, drives and needs.
- Behaviour can reflect a motive in a very subtle or disguised way.
- The same behaviour can reflect different motives at different times or in different people.
- People may be more or less aware of the forces guiding their behaviour and the conflicts driving them.
- Behaviour is governed by an energy system, with a relatively fixed amount of energy available at any one time.
- The goal of behaviour is pleasure (reduction of tension, release of energy) – the pleasure principle.
- People are driven primarily by sexual and aggressive instincts.

timeline

1901	1908
Freud, *The Psychopathology of Everyday Life*	Freud writes about anal eroticism

- The expression of these drives can conflict with the demands of society – so the energy that would be released in the fulfilment of these drives must find other channels of release.
- There is both a life (*eros*) and a death (*thanatos*) instinct.

Two things need to be said before the psychosexual theory is described. *Firstly*, people have three levels of awareness: conscious (what we are aware of), pre-conscious (what we can be aware of if we attend to it carefully) and unconscious (that about which we cannot be aware except under exceptional circumstances). Therapy is often aimed precisely at bringing the unconscious into the conscious.

Secondly, personality has a structure. It is the result of three factors: the unconscious, ever-present *id* that is the biological basis of personality; the partly conscious *ego* that develops in the first year and is the psychological executive of personality; the *superego* that develops from the age of 3 to 5 years and is the social and moral component of personality.

Freud's theory of the psychosexual stages posits four stages – oral, anal, phallic, genital – with each characterized by a particular erotogenic zone that is the primary voice of pleasure. The theory postulates that problems moving from one stage to the next lie at the heart of adult personality. If one moves through the state without any crises, fixations or regressions, it does not mark or influence adult personality. However, problems arising from these stages mark, influence or shape one for life. Hence there are adult personality traits that arise from childhood experiences. Further, opposite patterns can be seen as reactions to the same problem.

Learning The theory asserts that we all pass through these stages and that they can and do characterize us for the rest of our lives. This is at the heart of Freudian personality theory. Thus whereas biological psychologists would see personality traits like extraversion–introversion being determined by physiological process, the Freudians see personality development as stemming from early and largely forgotten childhood experiences. Thus, theoretically if somewhat unethically, one could shape a child's personality by what you do to them early in childhood.

> **It has been found that in early childhood there are signs of bodily activity to what only an ancient prejudice could deny the name of sexual.**
> **Sigmund Freud, 1920**

1949	**1968**	**1980**
Blum does first large scale studies on psychosexual development	Kline starts work on the anal character	Kline develops questionnaire to measure oral and anal types

Traits of psychosexual stages of development

	Abnormal	Normal	Abnormal
Oral traits			
	optimism	←——→	pessimism
	gullibility	←——→	suspiciousness
	manipulativeness	←——→	passivity
	admiration	←——→	envy
	cockiness	←——→	self-belittlement
Anal traits			
	stinginess	←——→	over-generosity
	constrictedness	←——→	expansiveness
	stubbornness	←——→	acquiescence
	orderliness	←——→	messiness
	rigid punctuality	←——→	tardiness
	meticulousness	←——→	dirtiness
	precision	←——→	vagueness
Phallic traits			
	vanity	←——→	self-hate
	pride	←——→	humility
	blind courage	←——→	timidity
	brashness	←——→	bashfulness
	gregariousness	←——→	isolation
	stylishness	←——→	plainness
	chastity	←——→	promiscuity
	gaiety	←——→	sadness

Orality The first phase, the oral, lasts up to about 18 months. The critical issue is about feeding and the erogenous zone is the mouth, lips and tongue. The issue is both about weaning from liquids onto solids but also about biting when the teeth arrive.

Children who have problems at this stage therefore become oral personalities because they are weaned too early or too late or have experienced oral deprivation or overindulgence. Many adult activities are very oral: eating, drinking, kissing, talking, smoking and chewing. The *deprived oral pessimist* may, according to the theory, use the mouth as a punishment. They may be very sarcastic and choose oral occupations like lawyer or dentist. Some will become food faddists, others drink prohibitionists. They may be speech purists, nail-biters or pen-chewers. They may enjoy particular Dracula movies or espouse the virtues of vegetarianism.

On the other hand, *indulgent oral optimists* may become sugar, wine or food experts or humorists. They are more likely to smoke, to play wind, rather than string or percussion, instruments and to like warm, milky and mild foods. Thus both oral optimists (indulged) and pessimists (deprived) live with their problems over early feeding but in very different ways.

Anality The second phase is the anal phase where the source of conflict is toilet training. It is about control: the child discovers he can control, please or frustrate parents by expelling or withholding faeces. Freudians believe this phase is associated with later hostile, sadistic and obsessive behaviour.

Anal traits are orderliness, parsimony and obstinacy. It has been suggested that attitudes to time, cleanliness and money are linked and associated with this phase. So the *anal eliminative* person is generous, untidy and chaotic, while the *anal retentives* are mean, meticulous and mindful. This is the world of petty officialdom, quality controllers and bankers. Then we have the ideas of anal fixation and anal eroticism which have bubbled down into popular language.

Phallic The phallic phase is characterized by the famous Oedipal (and Electra) complex. The erogenous zone is the genitals and this lasts from age two to five years. Freud regarded this as the kernel of neuroses. The 5-year-old boy supposedly (and unconsciously) feels both profound love for his mother and hatred of his father. But no society can tolerate incest and this leads to the castration complex, the belief that the father revenges the child's jealous rage by castration, which nullifies the complex.

The phase is characterized by either vanity or recklessness in adulthood or its opposite. So a poor resolution to this conflict may lead either to excessive promiscuity or to chastity. It may lead to parent fixation or continuously looking to the past. Pride and doubt, boldness and timidity are personality characteristics associated with the phallic stage.

The phallic stage is followed by *latency* and then the *genital stage*, which occurs from adulthood onwards. The sources of conflict are manifold and concern many of the difficulties experienced by all people: establishing healthy relationships, getting a job, enjoying life. It's about finding what the Freudians called adapted and healthy defence mechanisms.

Critique

Freudian ideas still attract disbelief, indignance and dismissal. Some have been put to the test and found wanting. Some researchers have demonstrated that aspects of the theory are certainly true. For over 50 years many of these ideas have been tested. There is some support for specific hypotheses but many have not stood up well against rigorous scientific experimentation. Whereas few psychologists appear to base any of their ideas or therapies on the psychosexual stages, many of the terms appear to be enthusiastically taken up by lay people.

the condensed idea
There are four stages of psychosexual development

39 Cognitive stages

'The existence of moral stages implies that moral development has a basic structural component, while motives and affects are involved in moral development these are largely mediated by changes in thought patterns.' Lawrence Kohlberg, 1973

Freud famously called children 'polymorphous perverts': the idea being that perversity can take many forms. All developmental psychologists face the daunting, if fascinating, task of explaining how irrational, illogical, egocentric babies develop into functioning, rational, logical adults. How is it that 8-year-olds can understand things 6-year-olds cannot? How do children learn to adapt to the world around them?

Probably the most famous and influential developmental psychologist was the French-speaking Swiss biologist, Jean Piaget. He developed a four-stage theory of cognitive development still discussed, debated and critiqued today.

Central concepts His central concern was how children learn to adapt to their world. The theory is about growth through adaptation and adjustment. It has a number of key concepts. The first is called *schemas*. A schema describes both the mental and physical actions involved in understanding and knowing the world. Schemas are categories of knowledge that help us to interpret and understand the world. A schema includes both a category of knowledge and the process of obtaining that knowledge.

timeline

1929	1932
Piaget, *The Child's Conception of the World*	Piaget, *The Moral Judgement of the Child*

With experiences, new information is used to modify, add to or change previously existing schemas. For example, a child may have a schema about a pet, such as a dog. If the child's sole experience has been with big dogs, they might believe that all dogs are big, boisterous and possibly aggressive. Suppose then that the child encounters a very small lap dog. The child will then take in this new information, modifying the previously existing schema to include this new knowledge.

The second concept is *accommodation*, which refers to how the individual changes or adjusts in order to deal with new ideas in the social and physical environment. The third concept is *assimilation*. The individual deals with the environment in terms of their cognitive schemas; that is, they deal with new information on the basis of the information that they have. They assimilate the old into the new.

This leads on to the fourth concept of *equilibrium*. As children progress through the stages of cognitive development, it is important to maintain a balance between applying previous knowledge (assimilation) and changing behaviour to account for new knowledge (accommodation). This process, called equilibration, explains how children are able to move from one stage of thought into the next. They are motivated to use new knowledge and skills to stop an unpleasant state of disequilibration. They resolve problems by moving on.

Four stages

1. **Sensorimotor stage** This stage lasts from birth to about 2 years of age. It is the stage of intelligence in action. The infant learns much knowledge by kicking, pulling and tweaking objects and moving around his or her environment. The key achievement is the concept of object permanence, which means the child is aware of the existence of objects when they are not in view.

2. **Preoperational stage** This stage lasts between the ages of about 2 and 7 years. It occurs with the development of language and play. Things are still partly magical and reality is not firm. Thinking during this stage is dominated by perception, and the child realizes that things are not

1966
Kohlberg's moral development theory first published

1971
Piaget, *Biology and Knowledge*

1980s
Doubts and critiques of Piaget begin

> *Knowing does not really imply making a copy of reality but rather, reacting to it and transforming it.*
>
> **Jean Piaget, 1971**

always the way they look. Children in this stage pay attention to only part of a given situation; this is called *centration*, which produces errors that have been shown in studies of conservation. Conservation refers to an understanding that certain aspects of an object remain the same in spite of various changes to it.

Famously, Piaget gave the child two glasses of the same size and shape containing the same quantity of liquid. When the child agreed there was the same quantity of water in both glasses, all the water from one of the glasses was poured into a glass that was taller and thinner. Preoperational children said either that there was more liquid in the new container ('because it's higher') or that there was more liquid in the original glass ('because it's wider') despite the fact it self-evidently contains the same fluid. The child centres, or focuses, only one dimension (height or width).

Preoperational children lack what is known as *reversibility*: the ability to undo mentally, or reverse, some operation that was carried out previously. Apart from too much reliance on perception, preoperational children also show egocentrism: assuming that their way of thinking about things is the only way.

3. **Concrete operations stage** This stage lasts between the ages of about 7 and 11 years. Here children's thinking becomes much less dependent on their perception and they are able to use a number of logico-mathematical operations. These operations include the actions indicated by common symbols such as $+$, $-$, $\div$, $\times$, $>$ (more than), $<$ (less than), and $=$. An operation such as 'greater than' should be considered together with 'less than'. A child has not grasped the meaning of 'A is greater than B' unless he or she realizes that this statement means the same as 'B is less than A'. However, in this phase the child's thinking is directed at concrete situations. The ability to escape from the limitations of immediate reality into the realm of abstract ideas is one that is found only in the fourth stage.

4. **Formal operations stage** Children from the age of 11 or 12 years enter the last developmental stage. In this stage, they develop the ability to think in terms of possible (rather than simply actual) states of the world. In other words, individuals in the stage of formal operations can manipulate ideas to a far greater extent than those in the concrete operations stage. For children in this stage, thought is always more

abstract, following the principles of formal logic. They can generate multiple hypotheses and generate abstract propositions and even do propositional logic with 'as-if' and 'if-then' steps.

Piaget's theory has of course received criticism, but it has been influential because it implies what children can learn at various stages because they are ready to learn. It also implies how children should be taught, particularly through the process of active self-discovery through toys and activities. The theory also articulates what a child should be taught.

Stages or sequences Nearly all stage-wise theories – whether they are cognitive/mental stages or adaptation to loss stages – make two crucial assumptions. The first is that stages are discrete rather than continuous. Stages imply the idea that they are quite distinct from one another and that what we might think, be able to do or believe at one stage is quite different from that of the last or the next. In developmental terms, this means those abilities or cognitive capacities that mark one stage are completely absent at previous stages.

The second is the concept of strict sequence. This means that one has to go through the phases or stages in a strictly prescribed order, neither skipping one nor, even more unlikely, regressing to an earlier period. Some proponents of psychological reactive stages have suggested that one can in fact 'go back' as well as forward. However, this is less the case in the cognitive development literature.

Certainly the evidence suggests that the cognitive development milestones or stages are not as neat or clear as theoreticians would like to claim but it is patently obvious that there is a developmental sequence. Seven-year-olds can master concepts that 4-year-olds cannot. Indeed, a great deal of educational practice and parenting advice is predicated on the concept of logical developmental stage-like sequences.

Current thinking

Current work on Piaget's cognitive stages suggests that he and some contemporary researchers underestimated children's abilities. Also current thinkers have said it is important to differentiate between performance (being able to do a task) and comprehension (knowing about something). It seems that when we test children they often have greater comprehension than performance ability, which has implications for testing the theory.

the condensed idea
Piaget's theory
of cognitive development

40 Ducks in a row

We read occasionally of animals who 'think' they are a different species. Of dogs believing they are cats; of sheep or pigs apparently acting more like dogs; even of ducks thinking they have human parents.

Lorenz The most famous psychological demonstration of this phenomenon is in the work of Konrad Lorenz (1907–89), a Nobel Prize winner and an important figure in ethology, the study of animal behaviour. He discovered that incubator-hatched greylag geese would 'imprint' on the first moving thing they saw, very specifically in the first 36 hours of life. He called the process 'stamping in', which in English is called imprinting. This specific time period has become known as the critical period. The goslings imprinted on Lorenz's black walking boots, and would follow him about as others would their mother. There are many charming pictures of him walking with them behind him or even swimming with his 'children'. Lorenz found that jackdaws who imprinted on him presented him with juicy worms (often in his ear-holes). However, thankfully, they sought out other jackdaws when sexually aroused; showing that some behaviours are more affected by imprinting than others. Ducklings would even imprint on inanimate objects like a red balloon and even a cardboard box.

Strictly, this phenomenon is called *filial imprinting*, where the new-born begins to recognize its parents. It even begins before birth as the new-born begins to hear the distinctive voice of its parents. The idea is that imprinting is innate and instinctive, not learned. It is essential for life and survival. But even innate behaviours are modified by learning. So cats are 'hard-wired' to catch rats but need to learn the art of rat-catching from

timeline

1000 BC	1871
Ancient farmers use imprinting for animal husbandry	Darwin writes about instinctual behaviour

their mother. Similarly, song birds can sing but they 'learn the tune' from those around them.

The modern view is that the imprinting process is much more 'plastic' and 'forgiving' than originally thought. To be an appropriate target (i.e. a 'mother' for social bonding), any animal or inanimate object has to be the provider of comfort.

Experimental imprinting Imprinting can involve the senses of sight, sound and smell. Essentially imprinting establishes an individual animal's preferences for a certain species. Further, the imprinting is stronger when the animal is under stress.

This concept has been used to help train orphaned birds (condors, eagles, geese) who did not have the opportunity to learn from their parents. So birds can be taught to behave as if a microlight aircraft is their parents and will follow it if necessary along traditional migrant routes.

Imprinting functions to provide recognition of kin, to help social attachment and mate selection. Animals must immediately recognize their parent, who needs to protect and feed them. It is a mechanism that ensures strong social bonds between offspring and parent.

Critical period

The critical period is sometimes called the sensitive period. It is a time-fixed period of early post-natal life. In ducks and geese it is 24–48 hours after hatching. In cats it is 2–7 weeks, in dogs 2–10 weeks and in primates 6–12 months.

Imprinting is the intersection between instinct and learning. It is not just learning. This idea is supported by three sorts of evidence. Firstly, the imprinting occurs only at a fixed, stringent time window. This is the critical period; learning after this period has different, weaker effects. Secondly, the imprinting process is irreversible – things are not forgotten, they are fixed. Thirdly, it is species specific. It happens to all animals in a particular species irrespective of other differences between them.

1900	1935	1957
Ethology as a science begins	Lorenz publishes an early paper on imprinting	Psychiatrists look at the imprinting of gender

> **Waterfowl, fostered by hens do not usually become sexually imprinted on chickens.**
>
> Konrad Lorenz, 1973

Sexual imprinting This is the idea that an animal starts developing sexual preference – i.e. choice of mates – based on the species they are imprinted on, rather than their own species, if different. Some observers have speculated that this could be, in part, an explanation for the many and often strange sexual fetishes that people show to materials like rubber or fur or indeed objects like shoes.

A reverse sexual imprinting pattern has been observed which has apparently evolved to suppress potentially disastrous inbreeding. This effect means that people who grow up together, in clear family units of domestic proximity, during the first few years of life (up to about 5–6 years) later seem particularly unattractive to each other sexually. On the other hand, children of opposite sex separated at birth often find each other particularly sexually attractive if they meet later on.

Imprinting in humans Imprinting in birds is well established. But in mammals it is rarer. Primates are born much more helpless and 'incomplete', with a very immature brain. The mother is the all-important provider and protector, caregiver and companion. The bonding and growing take place over longer periods of time.

Imprinting in human partners People often remark that their friends seem attracted to similar 'types'. A male friend might always seem to have short, dark-haired girlfriends; or a female friend constantly chasing tall, freckled males. Since Freud's later work it has been suggested that we maybe particularly attracted to (or even repelled by) those who remind us of our parents. The idea is an imprinting concept: early exposure to particular parental characteristics affects later adult mate preference.

Daughters of older fathers choose older partners; children of mixed-race marriages are more likely to choose a partner of their opposite race rather than the same-race parent. Hair and eye colour have also been investigated.

> **In older married couples, one often discovers features which give man and wife the semblance of brother and sister; in the same way, one might notice in a master and dog who have spent some time together likenesses in manner which are touching and comical at the same time.**
>
> Konrad Lorenz, 1954

Phase-stage learning

It certainly seems that there are critical periods for learning in a person's life and the term 'imprinting' is used to describe any kind of learning that occurs at a particular life stage. Thus there is accumulating evidence that there are critical periods for second language learning. The period up to 5 years old seems to be the best for fluent acquisition of other languages. Thus if any (rare and unfortunate) person is not exposed to any language before they reach puberty, they seem never to really be able to properly acquire the syntax of their 'mother tongue' later in life. The 'biological window of opportunity' argument for second language learning is much disputed. Some believe the critical period is only true for pronunciation, others both syntax and vocabulary.

Some have speculated that there may even be a critical period for the acquisition of, and certainly a preference for, musical skills and composition. Further, the acquisition of social skills and emotional intelligence seems to indicate the critical period around puberty.

People do choose partners who resemble their opposite-sex parent over and above the effects of their own or same-sex parent. And people choose those of similar eye and hair colour.

This human imprinting effect is a form of social learning. It certainly is not clear that it happens at a specific stage/age or that it occurs for everyone. It does not necessarily have to occur in infancy.

When people are free to do as they please, they usually imitate each other.
Eric Hoffer, 1955

the condensed idea
Baby ducks literally learn to 'love the one they're with'

41 *Tabula rasa*

'One of the most fundamental tenets of Marxism and of communist doctrines is that the personalities of people are shaped by their economic class and by their role in the class struggle which is about as environmentalistic a position as can be imagined.' George Albee, 1982

The *tabula rasa* or blank-state hypothesis is that people are born with no genetic, innate or evolutionary content or processes that develop, or come out, over time. Rather they are a blank state, an empty disk, onto which writing or data are stored so that their personal experiences determine who they are, what they become and what they believe.

History Both Aristotle and St Thomas Aquinas appeared to favour this radical 'nurture' or 'environmental' school of thinking, as opposed to the 'nature' or 'hereditarian' school. Opposed to this idea was the essentially Platonic school that favoured the idea of the human mind or spirit 'pre-existing' in some developed form in the heavens. The modern concept is mainly derived from the 17th-century English empirical philosopher John Locke, who saw the mind at birth as empty, blank and free from any knowledge or processes for acquiring and storing it, but also free from predetermined or innate drives. In this sense people are free to create their own destiny and identity. They are thus captains of their ship, masters of their fate, authors of their own mind . . . and destiny.

'Train up a child in the way he should go; and when he is old, he will not depart from it.'
Proverbs

To some extent the *tabula rasa* debate has been characterized as an either/or nature vs nurture debate. It has torn psychology apart with powerful movements like the eugenics movement,

timeline

300 BC	1700
Aristotle defines the concept	Locke's idea of the 'free author'

which were strong advocates of the anti-*tabula rasa* tradition. Indeed there has been something of a pendulum swing between extreme positions. Thus gender identity, homosexuality, etc., have been seen as almost exclusively genetically determined or totally 'socially constructed'.

Many argue that it is impossible to separate nature and nurture. Still, the free will vs determinism debate is often in the background of the *tabula rasa* debate.

Beliefs about human nature Jeremy Bentham (1748–1832) described man as a rational being, making choices and decisions in terms of enlightened self-interest. Gustave Le Bon (1841–1931) on the other hand, stressed the irrationality and impulsiveness of men in crowds. Thomas Hobbes (1588–1679) viewed man as selfish, nasty and brutish, whose strivings had to be restrained by a powerful government. Jean Jaques Rousseau (1712–78) saw the restraints of his civilization as the force that was destroying the nobility of natural man, the 'noble savage'.

> **The first messages written on the *tabula rasa* may not necessarily be the most difficult to erase.**
> **Jerome Kagan, 1976**

Experimental and social psychologists have attempted to spell out the determinants, structure and consequences of various 'philosophies of human nature'. One psychologist argued that there were six basic beliefs (and their opposites) about human nature. First, that people are (or are not) basically trustworthy, moral and responsible. Second, that people can control their outcomes and that they understand themselves, or lack self-determination and are irrational. Third, that people are altruistic, unselfish, and sincerely interested in others, or the opposite. Fourth, that people are able to maintain their beliefs in the face of group pressures to the contrary, or else give in to pressures of group and society. Fifth, that people are different from each other in personality and interests and that people can change over time, or are not changeable over time. Sixth, that people are complex and hard to understand, or are simple and easy to understand. These can be reduced to two dimensions: positive–negative (strength of will, trust, independence and altruism) and multiplexity (variability and complexity), which are by-and-large independent of one another.

> **The thief and the murderer follow nature just as much as the philanthropist.**
> **T.H. Huxley, 1873**

19th century	1960s	2002
Eugenics as cause of all behaviour	*Tabula rasa* environmentalism has its heyday	Pinker, *The Blank Slate*

Nature has always had more power than education.
Voltaire, 1739

Biology, evolution and the blank state The clearest and most vocal objection to the *tabula rasa* position has come from the evolutionary psychologists. They scorn the *tabula rasa*, noble savage myth, which they see as driven by political imperatives, not scientific fact. People who fear or dislike the concepts of determinism or of inequality, or both, reject the overwhelming and powerful evidence of evolution.

The evolutionary psychology position is very clear: the human being (body and mind) has been designed by natural selection to behave in particular ways. The brain is the product of evolutionary adaptation. We are 'hard-wired' and in this sense 'fated' to behave in particular ways. We remain 'naked apes'. Thus we all have a 'sweet tooth' in infancy for good reason.

The argument is that mate selection is essentially about reproductivity. We are primed to seek out people who will help us create healthy children and hence ensure the continuation of our genes. So men find women attractive by virtue primarily of their child-bearing ability. Body size (body mass index) and shape (waist-to-hip ratio and leg-to-body ratio), are all fundamentally important signals of fecundity. Males are 'programmed' to seek out indicators of youth and health. Hence they rate big eyes, clear skin, symmetry, blondness (for Caucasions only) as important. Women, on the other hand, look for signs of health, dominance and wealth. Hence they seek tall men with broad shoulders and chests but small waists. They are attracted to deep voices and signs of social intelligence. Wealth is also important because females see it as providing resources to look after young children.

The politics of human nature

Political writings express both explicit and implicit beliefs as to the origins of human nature. Thus it seems that communism must assume that selfish, competitive and self-aggrandisement aspects of human nature are not natural but the product of social economic and political conditions. Likewise, liberalism seems to assume that all people have a strong desire for total freedom, while conservatives have a negative view of man, believing people to be naturally selfish, aggressive and anarchic.

Are beliefs about the characteristics of human nature strongly related to a person's political orientation in predictable and logical ways? For example, left-wingers tend to attribute the origin of most human characteristics to the environment, and right-wing people to genetic factors, though there are vast differences depending on the characteristics considered (e.g. personality vs physical characteristics). Thus, it may be possible to determine a person's political orientation by asking his or her views on the nature–nurture issue, or vice versa.

> **"Give me a dozen healthy infants, well-formed, and my own specified world to bring them up in and I'll guarantee to take any one at random and train him to become any type of specialist I might select – doctor, lawyer, artist, merchant-chief and, yes, even beggar-man and thief, regardless of his talents, penchants, tendencies, abilities vocations and race of his ancestors."**

J. Watson, 1930

For the evolutionary psychologist we are designed to detect mating quality. Men unconsciously are attracted to women at the peak of their reproduction potential. In the evolutionary psychological scheme, women solved their 'detection problem' by evolving a preference for high status (particularly in long-term relationships) over other considerations like attractiveness. This is because, the higher a man is in status, the greater his ability to control resources. High status in most societies is associated with wealth and power; it may also be associated with intelligence, emotional stability, and conscientiousness, which are themselves desirable traits. Consequently, rivalry among men to attract women focuses on acquiring and displaying cues of resources. In men, then, beauty may only be 'wallet deep' as some have sardonically suggested.

Men, on the other hand, solved the problem of detecting peak reproductive potential in women by favouring features that signal high reproductive potential, youth or fertility rather than attributes that signal, say status. These features include full lips, clear skin, smooth skin, clear eyes, lustrous hair, good muscle tone and body fat distribution, with a bouncy youthful gait, an animated facial expression and a high energy level. While both men and women may value the same characteristic in a partner (such as attractiveness, status, emotional stability and so on), they weight these characteristics differently as a result of their evolutionary endowments.

the condensed idea
Are our minds
blank slates at birth?

42 Stay hungry

'I trust that I shall not be thought of as rash if I express a belief that experiments on the higher nervous activities of animals will yield not a few directional indications for education and self education in man.' I. Pavlov, 1928

The ability and apparent willingness of circus animals to perform tricks to the 'commands' of trainers used to fascinate our parents and grandparents. People still enjoy seeing seals, dolphins and even killer whales perform in large, public aquariums. The question is, how can animals be trained to perform such interesting and amazing tasks?

Dogs and bells The conditioned reflex was discovered by the Nobel Prize winning Russian physiologist Ivan Pavlov (1849–1936). His concept has become part of folklore because of the famous example of 'Pavlov's dogs'. All animals salivate when hungry and when presented with the sight or smell of a favoured food. This is a natural reflex designed to facilitate the whole process of eating and digesting food. Pavlov initially operated on dogs to measure the quality and quantity of their salivation to prepare food for effective digestion.

Pavlov found that if you rang a bell many times immediately after the dog saw the meat, the bell alone, without the sight of meat, would do the trick. The bell on its own set into motion the physiological digestive system. The process works with people, with all food and with many different sounds. Conditioning works better if the unconditioned stimulus (the food) occurs almost simultaneously with the conditioned stimulus (the bell) and when both stimuli are strong and intense (a big, juicy steak and a very loud bell).

The theory A conditioned reflex occurs under particular conditions when what is called an indifferent (or irrelevant) stimulus is paired or

timeline

1870s	1940s
Pavlov demonstrates conditioning	Skinner extends the idea significantly

combined with a particular stimulus that usually produces a specific response. After repeating this action for some time, the indifferent stimulus has the power, on its own, to produce that particular response. This is the conditioned stimulus that causes the reflex: the indifferent stimulus that provokes the conditioned response. To preserve the reflex, the association needs to be topped up; if the bell sounds again and again but without the presence of meat, the response is less likely to occur. So:

- the food is an unconditioned stimulus
- the salivation in response to the food is an unconditioned reflex
- the sound of the bell is the conditioned stimulus
- the salivation to the stimulus of the bell alone is the conditioned reflex.

The conditioned response may be to excite and increase the likelihood of a behaviour or the opposite, to try to inhibit that behaviour. The results are clear and commonsensical: the strength of the conditioning increases with every trial but each trial adds less strength than the trial before it. Put another way, after a while the power of reinforcement declines.

> **He that spareth his rod hateth his son.**
> **Proverbs**

Extinction

But conditioning can change. It can be undone as easily as it can be done. This can occur through what has been called experimental extinction and happens as a result of reinforced trials. Over time, if the food never followed the bell, the dog would cease to salivate at the sound of the bell. But if the salivatory response disappears it can be reconditioned by the return to the conditioning situation. In fact, even after apparent extinction it does not take long to resurrect once the reinforcement trials reoccur. Further, an extinguished response may appear again after a rest interval. This is called spontaneous recovery.

1944	1958	1969
Beginnings of focus on punishment	Systematic desensitization introduced	Jahoda, *The Psychology of Superstition*

Conditioned superstitions There is a famous story that illustrates what psychologists called 'superstitious behaviour'. An animal psychologist had a lab full of pigeons. Pigeons demonstrated they could recognize and discriminate between different shapes and colours. They had become quite used to the old 'food-for-a-correct-answer' routine.

One weekend, the researcher went home but forgot to turn off the time feeders for a row of birds. So after half an hour the machine dispensed a tasty helping of feed. Naturally, to the birds it appeared they had been rewarded for what they were doing. And then they repeated the behaviour every 30 minutes and out came the reward. Every so often the birds got ready to 'do their thing'. Some pecked at their cage, others lifted both wings, some pirouetted at the bottom of the cage, still others cooed appreciatively. The food came unconditionally, but the pigeons had 'seen connections' and causal links and believed they had brought about their just reward.

> **It is obvious that the different kinds of habits based on training, education and discipline of any sort are nothing but a long chain of conditioned reflexes.**
>
> **I. Pavlov, 1928**

In another famous study of children aged 3–6 years, the experimenters placed a plastic box for holding marbles and a child-sized mechanical clown named Bobo. At the beginning of the experiment, each child was allowed to choose a small toy that he or she wanted to win. They were then introduced to Bobo and told that, from time to time, the clown would dispense a marble, which the child should place in the plastic box. When enough marbles were collected, the child would earn the toy. Bobo was programmed to dispense marbles on a fixed schedule, regardless of the child's behaviour. Children were observed through a two-way mirror for one 8-minute session per day for six days. Results showed that 75 per cent of the children developed a distinctive superstitious response. Some children stood in front of Bobo and grimaced at him; others touched his face or nose; still others wiggled or swung their hips. One girl smiled at Bobo, and another kissed his nose. In each case, the children exhibited these behaviours repeatedly across several sessions. They all believed their actions produced the marbles. They had been classically conditioned.

The power of music Advertisers know that people associate particular tunes with particular events, moods and products, which change the probability of their purchasing behaviour. Indeed people may be influenced by musical cues without ever being clearly aware of the music in the background.

In one musical study psychologists played traditional French (accordion) music or traditional German music (a Bierkeller brass band – 'oompah') at customers and watched the sales of wine from their experimental wine shelves, which contained French and German wine matched for price and flavour. On French music days 77 per cent of the wine sold was French; on German music days 73 per cent was German. People were three or four times more likely to choose a wine that matched the music than wine that didn't match the music.

Conditioned fear   Classical conditioning influences emotion as well as behaviour. One can condition an animal to respond to a signal but soon suppress the response by associating it also with some nasty event like an electric shock or a shower of cold water. At the human level it has been possible to induce and cure phobic responses by conditioning. Thus one could make a small child phobic about cats by ensuring that every time they hear, see or touch a cat a loud noise sounds. This should quite quickly result in 'felinophobia'. However, this can be extinguished by introducing the child gradually to a cat that provides rewarding stimuli.

Systematic desensitization was first described by the neo-behaviourist Joseph Wolpe (1958) and found useful for clients who can identify a specific focus for their anxieties, such as a fear of closed rooms, or of speaking in public. Clients are asked to imagine anxiety-producing scenes that relate specifically to these concerns while the therapist helps them maintain a state of relaxation. The pairing of relaxation and the confrontation of anxiety decreases these fears through the process of 'reciprocal inhibition'. If clients can maintain a state of relaxation in the face of the anxiety-arousing stimuli, the stimuli will lose their potency.

> **‘Learning without thinking is useless. Thinking without learning is dangerous.’**
> Confucius, 551–479 BC

the condensed idea
Responses can be learned

43 Behaviourism

'The behaviourist sweeps aside all medieval conceptions. He drops from his vocabulary all subjective terms such as sensation, perception, image, desires, and even thinking and emotion.' **J.B. Watson**, 1926

History of behaviourism

Behaviourism was a dominant force in psychology for over 100 years. From Ivan Pavlov (1849–1936) to B.F. Skinner (1904–90), who denied that people had free will or moral autonomy, behaviourism in slightly different forms dominated psychological thinking and research for 50 years.

Behaviourists were the great enemies of the gestalt psychologists, the psycho-analysts and the humanistic psychologists. Early behaviourists like John B. Watson abandoned what they called 'introspection'.

Behaviourism was the science of (only) what you can observe and reliably measure: behaviour. It celebrated naïve empiricism.

Behaviourism is an ideology (like many 'isms') with core criteria, beliefs or axioms. We need observable behavioural evidence to demonstrate theories. Thus we cannot know or distinguish between two states of mind (attitudes, beliefs, values, etc.) unless we can observe and measure the specific behaviour associated with each.

Philosophy The philosophical origins of behaviourism lie in various philosophical movements like logical positivism and British empiricism. Logical positivists insisted on the principle of verification, which argues that mental concepts in fact refer to behavioural tendencies and so can and must be specified in behavioural terms. British empiricists insisted that we understand the world through experiment and observation (only). They

timeline

1913
Watson advocates behaviourism

1927
Pavlov provides core ideas

also believed that people acquire knowledge of their environment and, indeed, other people by associative learning between experiences (or stimuli) and ideas (or behaviours). Hence people understand the causal structure of the world through classical associations.

Behaviourists who claim their psychology is *the* psychology of behaviour (definitely not the science of the mind, the heart or the soul) argue that we can understand psychological processes without any reference to internal mental events like beliefs or memories. They argue, fiercely, that all internal-state language be totally eradicated from psychology to be replaced by strictly behavioural concepts. Behaviourism wants to be seen as a natural science like physics or zoology.

Naturally over the years there have been slightly different versions. There is *classical* or physiological behaviourism. This has developed its own language. So if dogs or rats are fed only after they perform a task – push a lever or move in a particular way when a sound occurs or a light gets switched on – they are likely to repeat this behaviour. So the sound or light is a discriminative stimulus, the movement or presses are responses, the food is reinforcement and the repeated actions are learning histories.

> **A scientific analysis of behaviour must, I believe, assume that a person's behaviour is controlled by his genetic and environmental histories rather than by the person himself as an initiating agent.**
>
> **B.F. Skinner, 1974**

Methodological behaviourism is the doctrine of how to do acceptable, empirical, scientific research. Internal mental events of all types are irrelevant private entities. Behaviourism often rejoices in the term 'the experimental analysis of behaviour'. Indeed societies and academic journals have been founded with this very name.

Perhaps more than anything else it is the *radical* behaviourism of B.F. Skinner that is best known. He was a true believer who wrote novels about behaviourist utopias and brought up his daughter according to the strict principles of his creed. Radical behaviourism would not allow for the existence and 'experimentation' of states of mind. But this version of behaviourism would not allow that feelings cause behaviour – rather that some behaviours could be manifestations of feelings.

1938
Skinner, *The Behaviour of Organisms*

1950s
High point of behaviourism

1977
Bandura, *Social Learning Theory*

Behaviourists tend to focus on very specific identifiable behaviours which they argue can be shaped by well-planned reinforcement schedules. But some are prepared to accept that we are more than simply products of our personal reinforcement history. We are also affected by our personal biological factors and in some instances by culture, which is in effect the common behaviours of our clan or group.

Behaviourists have formed societies and founded learned journals. They have recommended a particular type of therapy inevitably called behaviour therapy. This has been used to treat mental patients and disturbed children as well as 'normal' adults with particular problems.

Beyond freedom and dignity
B.F. Skinner – perhaps the best known, most vocal and clearest thinking behaviourist – wrote a popular book *Beyond Freedom and Dignity* in 1971. Skinner hated the mentalists, who believed in a *homunculus* or 'little person' (perhaps the mind or will or soul) in the head.

Skinner's behaviourism is determinist and technological. Further, he believed behaviourism can be a force for good, helping to solve social problems like overpopulation, war, etc. He wanted us to drop all obscure and unhelpful talk of personal freedom and of dignity because that is, in his view, false thinking.

Skinner did not believe in free will and the idea therefore that people can or should take credit for certain actions or blame for others. All our behaviour is shaped by our past history of reinforcement. He did not believe in punishment because that assumes people may have free choices about their behaviour. If we see a person coached or compelled or constrained to behave in a particular way, we believe that they are less worthy of praise or blame because they have less free will. Yet all our behaviours are shaped this way.

Skinner rejected the idea of behaviourism as black-box or 'empty organism' psychology. But he is clear that we are products of our environment, our learning and more specifically our reinforcement schedule.

Social learning theory
Albert Bandura (b.1925) developed social cognitive theory or social learning theory, which is a development of pure or radical behaviourism. Like all behaviourists he stresses the role of social learning, believing that we can only really understand (and therefore predict) a person's behaviour when we take full account of the social and physical context or environment in which they find themselves by choice or accident.

There are various important concepts. The first is *observational learning* or modelling. The idea is that we often learn by observing and then imitating others who act as models. So we obtain vicarious reinforcement when we see others rewarded or punished for what they do. Hence the power of television and films to encourage behaviour change through the use of attractive, trustworthy actors doing particular things for specific rewards.

Central to social learning theory is the idea of *self-efficacy*, which is an individual's belief concerning their ability to cope or achieve in a particular situation or with a particular task. The evaluation of self-efficacy in any situation is a function of four things: their learning history or success and failure in similar situations; salient vicarious experiences (knowledge of how others behave in similar situations); verbal/social persuasion or reinforcement or the extent to which others have encouraged or persuaded them to act in that situation; and emotional arousal or the feelings of anxiety or distress associated with possible failure. Self-efficacy judgements play an important role in motivation, goal-setting, etc., at school and work and in therapy. The more people believe they know what to do, have had experience of success and want to avoid failure, the more likely they aim to succeed.

A final concept is *self-regulation*, which means using thoughts/beliefs to control behaviour. These are personal resources which are a way of self-rewarding and punishing behaviour. It results from people observing their own behaviour and judging how it occurs and how it compares to others'. People react with pleasure and pride to success, and pain and self-criticism to failure. Self-regulation processes mean that they tend to repeat things that increase their feelings of self-worth or self-esteem and avoid those that lead to self-defeat and self-loathing. Self-regulation encourages people to set standards which they can achieve and which in turn increase their sense of self-efficacy. So internal factors – self-observation, self-reactive, self-reinforcement – are seen to be motivating forces.

> **Behaviourism could be accurately and briefly described as psychology which leaves out psychology.**
>
> **G.D. Martin, 1976**

the condensed idea
Behaviour is influenced by experience

44 Reinforcement schedules

'I could not have predicted that among the reinforcers which explain my scientific behaviour the opinions of others would not rank high, but that seems to be the case.'
B.F. Skinner, 1967

Reinforcement in psychology means to strengthen a response. It is the major 'weapon' in the armoury of animal trainers. An animal, be it a jungle elephant, a circus lion or an experimental white rat, may be given a tasty morsel after a particular action or behaviour. The food is a reinforcer. Its aim is to encourage the animal to repeat the act as frequently and quickly as possible under the same conditions. A reward, whatever it is, can be justified on its reinforcing power exclusively by how quickly and regularly it changes behaviour after it is received.

Different reinforcers Behaviourists make distinctions between different types of reinforcers. So there are *primary* reinforcers (food, sex) that all animals want and need throughout their lives. Their power depends on their state (how hungry, sleep-deprived, etc. they are). *Secondary* reinforcers occur with learning to pair a behaviour with a response: a dinner gong with salivation; the smell of disinfectant with hospitals. All sorts of things can become secondary reinforcers. Some, like money, are very general, others (a particular sound or smell, for example) are very specific. It is possible to establish a reinforcement hierarchy for an individual (or a species) showing the relative power of different reinforcers.

Trainers, leaders and managers put people on a reinforcement schedule. When complex responses are desired, 'shaping' is sometimes useful. This involves positively reinforcing responses that are part of the more complex one until the desired response is obtained.

Motivational techniques from learning theory

Procedure	At work	Behavioural effect
Positive reinforcement	Manager compliments employee when work is completed on time	Increases desired behaviour
Negative reinforcement	Manager writes a warning each time work is handed in late	Increases desired behaviour
Punishment	Manager increases employee workload each time work is handed in late	Decreases undesired behaviour
Extinction	Manager ignores the employee when work is handed in late	Decreases undesired behaviour

People learn to engage in behaviours that have positive results and actions that are pleasurable. The process by which people learn to perform acts leading to desirable outcomes is known as *positive reinforcement*. For a reward to serve as a positive reinforcer, it must be made contingent on the specific behaviour sought.

People also learn to perform acts because they permit them to avoid undesirable consequences. Unpleasant events, such as reprimands, rejection, firing, demotion and termination, are some of the consequences faced for certain actions in the workplace. The process is known as *negative reinforcement*, or *avoidance*.

Punishment involves presenting an undesirable or aversive consequence in response to an unwanted behaviour. Whereas negative reinforcement removes an aversive stimulus, thereby increasing the strength of the response that led to its removal, punishment applies an aversive stimulus, thereby decreasing the strength of the response that led to its presentation.

The link between a behaviour and its consequences may also be weakened via the process of *extinction*. When a response that was once rewarded is no

1967	1974	1994
Argyle uses the word 'rewardingness' in social psychology	Skinner, *About Behaviorism*	Kohn, *Punished by Rewards*

longer rewarded, it tends to weaken; it will gradually die out. Ignoring requests and behaviour is probably the most common way of extinguishing it.

Contingencies of reinforcement The four reinforcement contingencies may be defined in terms of the presentation or withdrawal of a pleasant or unpleasant stimulus. Positively or negatively reinforced behaviours are strengthened; punished or extinguished behaviours are weakened.

Stimulus presented or withdrawn	Desirability of stimulus	Name of contingency	Strength of response	Business example
Presented	Pleasant	Positive reinforcement	Increases	Praise from a supervisor encourages continuing the praised behaviour
	Unpleasant	Punishment	Decreases	Criticism from a supervisor discourages enacting the punishment behaviour
Withdrawn	Pleasant	Extinction	Decreases	Failing to praise a helpful act reduces the odds of helping in the future
	Unpleasant	Negative reinforcement	Increases	Future criticism is avoided by doing whatever the supervisor wants

There are essentially four types of reinforcement schedule.

Fixed interval schedules are those in which reinforcement is administered the first time the desired behaviour occurs after a specific amount of time has passed. Rewards are administered on a regular, fixed basis. Fixed interval schedules are not especially effective in maintaining desired job performance, although they are widely used.

Variable interval schedules are those in which a variable amount of time must elapse between the administration of reinforcements. For example, an auditor who pays surprise visits to the various branch offices on an average of every 8 weeks (e.g. visits may be 6 weeks apart one time, and 10 weeks apart another) is using a variable interval schedule. Because the employee cannot tell exactly when they will be rewarded, they will tend to perform well for a relatively long period.

Fixed ratio schedules are those in which reinforcement is administered the first time the desired behaviour occurs after a specific number of such actions have been performed. Any type of piecework pay system constitutes a fixed ratio schedule of reinforcement.

Variable ratio schedules are those in which a variable number of desired responses (based on some average amount) must elapse between the administration of reinforcements. The classic example of the effectiveness of variable ratio schedules is playing one-armed bandit (slot/gambling) machines.

A standard critique of the concept is that it is circular: response strength is increased by things which increase response strength. However, defenders point out that reinforcers are such because of their effect on behaviour (and not the other way around).

Punished by rewards Do children do better at school if reinforced by gold stars, prizes or even monetary rewards? Do incentive plans increase productivity at work? Is it better to praise than pay for performance?

Some studies have shown that if you reward students for problem-solving they are slower than non-rewarded students; that creative artists are less creative when commissioned; that people who are rewarded for sensible behaviour like stopping smoking or wearing seatbelts are less likely to change their behaviour in the long term than those not rewarded.

Against the major principles of reinforcement, Alfie Kohn argues that the more you reinforce a person for any activity (productivity, academic marks, creativity), the more they will lose interest in the very activity they are being rewarded for. That is, extrinsic motivation (getting a reward) reduces intrinsic motivation (the fun of the activity).

Kohn argues that reward systems can be cheap (e.g. gold stars), easy to administer, and appear to yield immediate effects, but in the long term they fail for a variety of reasons.

There is considerable dispute as to whether the now vast academic, experimental literature essentially supports Kohn's position or not. The debate rumbles on but it has made people think seriously about the use and possible abuse of reinforcement schemes at school and work.

> **It is likely that response to an infant's cries does more than reinforce crying. It reinforces active coping with the environment, reaching out to obtain feedback from people and objects.**
>
> L. Yarrow, 1975

the condensed idea
Behaviour is shaped
by its consequences

45 Mastering complexity

'There is a tendency to define psychology in what strikes me as a curious, and basically unscientific way, as having to do only with behaviour or only with processing of information only with certain low level-types of interaction with the environment . . . and to exclude from psychology the study of what I call competence.' N. Chomsky, 1977

Until around the 1960s psychology was divided by a triumvirate: the old-fashioned psychoanalysts; the 'brave new world' behaviourists; and splinter-party humanists. But the 1960s saw the start of a movement that was to last till the end of the century: the cognitive revolution. It started primarily because the behaviourists seemed to have a quite inadequate account of how we master higher-level skills: how we talk, how we reason, how we learn.

Observational learning Whereas the behaviourists insisted that we learn practically everything through operant conditioning, social learning theorists argued that we also learn quickly and effectively through observation. We expand our knowledge and skill by closely observing others (models). Children and adults quite obviously learn things vicariously by watching what other people do and the consequence of their actions.

For instance, many people worry what children 'pick up' from the television. They worry that children copy what they see: bad language, aggression, selfishness. Curiously however, they seem not to be so concerned with using television to teach virtues and good behaviour. Children copy both aggressive and altruistic models.

timeline

1960	1965
Bandura demonstrates observational learning	Chomsky starts a language revolution

In a celebrated study using a doll, young children were divided into three groups. They each saw a film in which an adult was aggressive towards an inflated doll, hitting it with a hammer, throwing it in the air and shouting comic-strip phrases like 'boom!', 'pow!' In the first condition another adult appears in the film and gives the actor sweets for his great performance; scolds and spanks the actor for behaving badly toward the doll; or does nothing. The 'experimental' children were then introduced to the same doll. As predicted, those who had seen the model rewarded for aggression were more likely themselves to be aggressive.

Implicit learning Can you learn without being aware that you are learning? Implicit learning is where people can be shown to have acquired complex information without being able to provide conscious recollection of what precisely they have learned.

Expertise

Many professionals develop a most impressive range of skills. Some of these are 'perceptual motor' skills like learning to play tennis to Wimbledon standard or 'learning' to become a chess grand master. There appear to be clear phases in the acquisition of these skills: a *cognitive* or understanding phase; then a *practice* or associative phase; and finally an *autonomous* phase where people become faster and more accurate.

Psychologists have studied experts in comparison with novices. Experts seems to have a very well organized store of knowledge or templates concerning possible events/positions/circumstances that have occurred in the past. They have clearly learnt to scan, search and evaluate situations very efficiently, almost unconsciously. Developing expertise takes more than simple talent and practice. It involves building up a store of procedural knowledge that is used to do things so well.

1980s	1990s	2000
Start of work on implicit learning	Studies on how people become experts	Developments in the cognitive neuropsychology of learning

There is some evidence that different parts of the brain are responsible for explicit as opposed to implicit learning. And it is still uncertain whether explicit learning is followed by implicit learning or the other way around. Hence we can talk about an explicit memory where people can give conscious verbal descriptions, in contrast to an implicit memory where they cannot. The difference is sometimes called declarative vs procedural memory. A good example is watching and talking to skilled and talented sports people who have learnt all sorts of clever physical moves but cannot articulate what they do.

Learning language Learning language is fundamental for survival. Yet mastering one's native or mother tongue is clearly a very complex process that is achieved by nearly all children with apparent ease.

The behaviourists argue that language is acquired just like any other behavioural repertoire. A child utters a word: if it is rewarded or reinforced, he or she repeats it. Children are strongly, constantly and enthusiastically rewarded by parents and caregivers by making successive approximations to accurate speech. Initially this starts with imitation by simple, classical behaviourist principles.

Studies show that indeed parents do take a great interest in their children's language development. However, they reward speech by whether it is judged as 'kind and truthful' as much as whether it is grammatically correct.

The problem with the behaviourists' theory is that children learn language too fast and too accurately for it to be based on principles of imitation and reinforcement. Children become creative with speech and often suddenly produce sentences that they have clearly never heard before. The theory clearly fails to explain the rapid development of complex grammatical rules. As is very apparent, parents do not spend a lot of time 'shaping the grammar' of their children yet they pick it up with astonishing speed.

It is mother–child interactions which seem most relevant and have been carefully studied. Many mothers talk to their children about daily events and familiar objects, often changing the topic of their monologues to the very specific objects that the child is paying attention to.

Mothers seem to start with 'motherese', which is the use of short, simple, very descriptive sentences. As the child grows older, the length and complexity of the sentences grow, with the mother always being 'ahead' of the child and so trying to teach and encourage. Despite all this help and both specific and non-specific reinforcement, it is not clear that this process accounts for language development around the world, with all languages and for all time.

Chomsky and deep structure   Over 50 years ago Noam Chomsky put forward a clear and very influential challenge to the behaviourist account. He proposed a 'nativist' theory which argues that children are born with the knowledge of the structure of human language. All human beings in all cultures have a natural language acquisition device.

Chomsky distinguished between *deep* and *surface* structure. Surface refers to an actual linguistic phrase, but deep to its meaning. So a sentence 'You will be lucky to get him to work for you' can have two meanings: 'You will be lucky if he chooses to work in your organization', or 'You will be lucky if you get him to do any work at all'. Similarly, we can have two different sentences (different surface structure) but which have the same meaning, that is deep structure. So, 'The old professor gave the lecture' means exactly the same as 'The lecture was given by the old professor'.

A related concept is that of *transformational grammar*, which is thought to be innate. This is the mechanism which allows us to express meaning correctly in words. Chomsky was able to show *linguistic universals* to support his theory. That is, all human languages share various common features: nouns, verbs and adjectives as well as vowels and consonants. This explains why children soon acquire any language to which they are exposed whether or not it is their parents' native language.

> **'Reaching out to obtain feedback from people and objects.'**
> L. Yarrow, 1975

The nativist explanation is that language learning depends on biological maturation. However, critics claim that this approach is more descriptive than explanatory. That is, it does not really give a detailed and precise account of how language acquisition really works. Also it is clear that children's personal experiences do affect their language development. It has been argued that language universals may simply reflect the fact that people face the same demands in all cultures and that it is this, rather than some inborn device, that really shapes language.

the condensed idea
Higher-level learning requires more than conditioning

46 Phrenology

'No physiologist who calmly considers the question [the truth of phrenology] . . . can long resist the conviction that different parts of the cerebrum subserve different kinds of mental action.' Herbert Spencer, 1896

Phrenology is based on a simple idea that is current today. The brain is the 'organ of the mind' and it is structured so that different parts are responsible for different functions. Therefore different parts of the brain that are reflected in the shape of the head control different facilities. But phrenologists believed, firstly, that the size of the brain area 'dedicated' to a particular function is proportioned in size to the 'importance' of that mental facility. Secondly, that craniometry (which is the measurement of things like skull size and shape) represents the form of the brain and therefore all human functions. Thirdly, that both moral and intellectual facilities are innate.

History The roots of phrenology go back at least to the ancient Greeks and probably further than that. Many practitioners have been essential physiognomists – readers of nature by the form of things. Many books on arts and science, particularly in the 17th and 18th centuries, showed pictures, silhouettes and drawings that illustrated physiognomic principles. The modern system was developed by Franz Gall, who published his treatise in 1819. He believed his brain map linked brain areas called organs with specific functions called faculties.

In 1896 Sizer and Drayton published a phrenology manual entitled *Heads and Faces, and How to Study Them*. It illustrated how to recognize idiots and poets as well as those with a criminal as opposed to moral character. To the modern eye it is somewhere between an amusing and bizarre treatise.

timeline

1810	1824
Gall develops the system	*Phrenology Journal* started

The Victorians really took phrenology seriously. Their busts, casts, journals, callipers and machines survive – particularly the fine white china busts produced by the London Phrenology Company. The Victorians had phrenological surgeries, schools, foods and doctors. They measured heads enthusiastically: head size meant brain size, which in turn meant mental power and temperament – or so they believed. The average man had apparently a head size of 22 inches and a woman ½ to ¾ inch less. Head size was linearly related to brain capacity and intellect except where people were hydroencephalic. But shape was more important than size. A good cranioscopy could, they believed, show special talents. Phrenologists made diagnoses and predictions about motives, abilities and temperament. In short, the head was the manifestation of the mind and the soul of an individual.

> **'Among neuroscientists phrenology now has a higher reputation than Freudian psychiatry, since phrenology was in a certain crude way a precursor to electro-encephalography.'**
>
> Tom Wolfe, 1997

Victorian phrenologists acted as talent-spotters. Some did cross-national comparisons, looking at English–French differences. Phrenologists examined skeletons like the skull and bones of Archbishop Thomas Beckett. Queen Victoria had her children 'read' because phrenologists professed both self-knowledge and the keys to developmental, moral and occupational success.

Various groups and individuals carried the torch for phrenology. These included Nazis and colonialists who wanted to use phrenological evidence of the superiority of certain groups. This has tainted phrenology ever since.

Reading the head The traditional 'reading of the head' begins by first considering the overall shape of the head. A rounded head supposedly indicates a strong, confident, courageous, sometimes restless nature. A square head reveals a solid, reliable nature, deeply thoughtful and purposeful. The wider head suggests an energetic, outgoing character, while the narrower head suggests a more withdrawn, inward-looking nature. An ovoid shape belongs to an intellectual. The phrenologist then gently but firmly runs their fingers over the skull in order to feel the contours of the skull. They have to measure individual size of each faculty and its

1838
S. Smith, *The Principles of Phrenology*

1902
Hollander, *Scientific Phrenology*

2000
London Phrenology Company china phrenology heads still sell well

prominence in comparison with other parts of the head. As the brain consists of two hemispheres, each faculty can be duplicated, so they check both sides of the skull.

A faculty that is underdeveloped in comparison to the others indicates a lack of that particular quality in the personality, while one that is well developed indicates that the quality is present to a considerable degree. So a small organ of 'alimentiveness' indicates a light and finicky eater, possibly a teetotaller; if this faculty is well developed, it indicates a person who enjoys food and wine; and if overdeveloped, a glutton, who may also drink to excess.

The phrenological head has over 40 regions but it depends on which list or system you read. Some have rather old-fashioned concepts, like 20 'Veneration', which is respect for society, its rules and institutions; 26 'Mirthfulness', which is cheerfulness and sense of humour, and

Sentiments and propensities

The areas of the head have been further described or classified into eight sentiments or propensities.

- The 'domestic' propensities are characteristics common to man and animals and are basically responsible for one's emotions and instinctive reactions to objects and events.

- The 'selfish' propensities provide for man's wants and assist him in self-protection and self-preservation.

- The 'self-regarding' sentiments are concerned with self-interest and expression of personality.

- The 'perceptive' faculties are responsible for awareness of surroundings.

- The 'artistic' propensities give rise to sensitivity and aptitude in art and artistic creation.

- The 'semi-perceptive' faculties in such fields as literature, music and language, are responsible for appreciation of cultural surroundings.

- The 'reflective', 'reasoning' and 'intuitive' faculties are concerned with styles of thinking.

- The 'moral' sentiments, including religious faculties, humanize and elevate the character.

24 'Sublimity', which is the love of grand concepts. There are also head regions for 1 'Amativeness' (sex appeal); 3 'Philoprogenitiveness' (parental, filial love); 10 'Alimentiveness' (appetite, love of food); 31 'Eventuality' (memory); and 5 'Inhabitiveness' (love of home).

Critique Despite phrenology's popularity, mainstream science has always dismissed it as quackery and pseudo-science. The idea that 'bumps' on the head are related to personality structure and moral development was dismissed as nonsense. The evidence has been evaluated and is wanting.

The rise of neuroscience has shown how many of the claims of phrenology are fraudulent. However, there remain other popular brain myths, such as the idea that we only use 10 per cent of our brain in day-to-day processing. There are also myths about brain energy, brain tuners and brain tonics which seem as plausible as phrenology.

However, there remain some aspects of phrenology that seem relevant today. We know for instance that brain size is positively correlated with mental ability test scores and within and between species. We also know that head size is correlated with brain size. In fact psychologists have demonstrated for nearly 100 years that there is a modest relationship between head size (length and breadth) and IQ. However, when corrected for body size this relationship drops and possibly disappears. Through use of sophisticated brain scanning, scientists have looked for evidence of the relationship between brain size and IQ. Again results are not that clear.

> **The notion that bumps on the skull correspond to overdeveloped areas of the brain is, of course, nonsense and Gall's scientific reputation was badly damaged by his phrenology.**
> R. Hogan and R. Smither, 2001

Certainly new technology has increased our knowledge of, and interest in, cognitive neuropsychology and psychiatry. We are now able to map the brain electronically and metabolically. Through studies both of accident victims as well as 'normal' people we are building up a new detailed map of the brain and what 'parts' are primarily responsible for what functions. But this 'electrophrenology' is empirically based and bears no relationship to the old, pre-scientific, moralistic ideas of the founders of phrenology.

the condensed idea
Some aspects of phrenology are still relevant today

47 Breaking up is hard to do

Most of us like to think of ourselves as cool, rational and objective people. We hopefully rejoice in data-based, analytical logic. We hope that we make wise, well-thought-through decisions throughout life. We are, we hope, 'people of the head'. We are warned not to let our heart rule our head. We are encouraged, in making big decisions, to 'sleep on it'. We are, of course, also people of the heart.

The idea of two sides to our personality and behaviour is very appealing. We have, after all, two eyes, two hands, two legs. We have two ears and two arms, and either two breasts or two testicles. Two of our most important organs seems to have two separate and separable halves. As a consequence it is a popular idea to talk of left versus right brain structure and functioning. This has been going on for hundreds of years. Laterality fascination led to many odd ideas and practices. Some thought the dual brain led to a dual personality. Others saw a good–bad dimension. So the right – being inferior to the left – was primitive, uncivilized and brutish. Then the left was seen to be the creative, feminine, initiative side bullied by the masterful right.

Part of the myth is associated with language. The Latin, Anglo-Saxon and French words for 'left' all imply negative features: awkward, clumsy, useless or weak, while the opposite is true for the associations of right, which is dextrous, correct and adroit.

Myth The idea is essentially this: the left brain is the logical brain. It is the hemisphere that processes facts, knowledge, order and patterns. It is the bit that does maths and science. It is the centre of detail-oriented abstract

timeline

1888	1960
First paper notes sex differences in hand shape (2D/4D ratio)	First split-brain operation

thinking and processing. The left-brain words are 'logical', 'sequential', 'rational', 'analytical', 'objective' and 'parts-orientated'. Most educational and business organizations have been set up by left-brained people to do left-brained things in a left-brained way. Just as the world is dominated by right-handers (dexters) – controlled, of course, by the left brain – so there is a quirky minority of people (around 10 per cent) who are left-handed because they are controlled by the right brain.

The right brain, it is said on the other hand, is all a bit fuzzy. It is the seat of emotions, symbols and images. It's where philosophy and religion are processed. It's big-picture territory; the zone of fantasy and possibilities. Right-brain words are 'random', 'intuitive', 'holistic', 'synthesizing' and 'subjective'. Right-brained students like the big picture: outline before details. They are, however, not too concerned with sequential planning or proof-reading or spelling or . . . other trivial details. They don't like symbols, but they shine at intuition. They like coherence and meaning, but are fantasy-based, not reality-based.

> **There is no reason to believe that the two hemispheres correspond to the distinction between rational vs intuitive thought, or analytic vs artistic processes or the difference between Western and Eastern philosophies of life.**
> H. Gleitman, 1981

The consultants, trainers and educators who espouse the 'two-brain' theory often talk of the split-brain experiment where the channel – the *corpus callosum* – between the hemispheres is severed. They also document studies where faces are 'reassembled' from two right or two left images. But they make a quick and (rather right-brained) imaginative and evidence-free jump from this to two-brain theory.

Split-brain research Split-brain operations were first performed in the 1960s to relieve intractable epilepsy. It allowed an investigation of the way each the two sides functioned without the interference of the other. Thus the left brain seemed able to do things the right brain could not (e.g. language) and vice versa. It seemed that much of the all-important language processing occurs in the left hemisphere but if this is damaged in children, some of these functions can be taken over by the right. Research in this area continues and is greatly helped by the new technologies we have to investigate brain functioning.

1970s	**1996**	**2002**
Popular books on left–right brain 'thinking, management, and creativity'	Academic journal *Laterality* founded	McManus, *Right Hand Left Hand*

The real brain scientists know that much of this left–right brain stuff is little more than metaphor. People are not left- or right-brained – but scientists do know that certain parts of the brain, sometimes located in the left hemisphere and sometimes in the right, do control different functions.

Laterality Strictly speaking laterality is about preference. We may be left or right eared, handed or footed. Overall, around 85–90 per cent of people are right-handed and right-footed but the numbers drop of those who favour the right eye and ear. Animals also show preferences, and true ambidextrousness is very rare. Mixed-handedness (cross-dominance) is certainly more common and it indicates people who choose to do different tasks more comfortably and accurately with one hand than with the other (write, play tennis or play the violin).

Because of the predominance of right-handers, the world has, it appears, been designed for them. So can-openers and scissors can prove a problem to left-handers. Eating with the right hand is a requirement in some cultures, and the rather complicated, beautiful Chinese calligraphy is difficult to do with the left hand. However, left-handers may have an advantage in certain sports, particularly in one-to-one sports where they are likely to face right-handers. They also have been very successful at duelling, partly because of the surprise factor that they can use.

There is a wide range of theories that attempt to account for the great differences in handedness, some with much more empirical support than others. There are evolutionary theories which argue that left-handers have survived because of their demonstrated advantage in combat. There are also environmental theories which associate left-handedness with birth stress. Sociological and anthropological theories refer the social stigma related to left-handedness and the repression of young left-handers by teachers and parents.

> **❝I believe myself able to prove – 1. That each cerebrum is a distinct and perfect whole as an organ of thought. 2. That a separate and distinct process of thinking or ratiocination may be carried on in each cerebrum simultaneously.❞**
>
> **A. Wigan, 1844**

But the current consensus is with genetic and biological theories which show quite clearly that handedness runs in families. They make an important distinction between natural, learned and pathological left-handers. All sorts of data, some very questionable, suggest that left-handedness is associated with very specific psychological problems like mental retardation as well as positive things like creativity. This has led to some unproven theories and the development of even more myths.

Body asymmetry

Body asymmetry has also been investigated. It is possible to measure what is called fluctuating asymmetry by measuring ankle and wrist width, ear length, finger and toe length and elbow breadth, noting differences within individuals. Various studies have shown lack of symmetry to be associated with ill-health. The more asymmetrical you are anywhere in your body, the more you are likely to have a wide range of problems. However, this area of investigation remains very preliminary.

Equally, there is increasing interest in sex differences in symmetry; notably the 2D/4D digit ratio discussed below, which shows systematic sex differences and which has been linked to many abilities and preference. Studies have looked at everything from choice of job, music and interests as they relate to a very simple measure of the difference in length between two fingers on each hand. Most controversially, this has been linked to sexual orientation, attractiveness and aggressiveness.

Males have a consistently smaller length ratio between their index (2D) and ring (4D) fingers compared with women. The idea is that finger length is a consequence of being 'washed with testosterone in the womb' (exposure to pre-natal androgens) which leads to more or less masculinization of the individual and which is manifest in everything from aggressiveness to preferences for homo- or heterosexual partners.

This fact has been known for well over 100 years but it is only in the last decade that research in this area has really taken off. It is an active and highly disputed area of research with many equivocal findings.

the condensed idea
Is split-brain theory correct?

48 Aphasia

Sometimes when very tired, or very upset or moderately drunk, people say they 'can't find the right word' for something they know well. Or equally, for no good reason they can't seem to understand what somebody is saying albeit in their own language. They maybe suffering from temporary mild aphasia.

Definition

Aphasia is a loss of the ability to produce and/or comprehend language, due to injury to brain areas specialized for these functions. In typical psychological jargon it has been defined as 'a multi-mortality reduction in the capacity to decide (interpret) and encode (formulate) meaningful linguistic elements that cause problems in listening, reading, speaking and wording'. In the 1880s it was proposed that aphasia was not just a loss of words but a loss of the ability to proportionize or use words for the purpose of conveying information. It is not a result of deficits in sensory, intellectual or psychiatric functioning, nor is it due to muscle weakness or a cognitive disorder.

Special problems   The term 'aphasia' often refers to a family of rather diverse communication disorders, mainly concerned with oral or written language. Thus, following brain damage, patients can have very specific problems like difficulties with reading but also possibly with writing. Some cannot complete spoken sentences because they can't retrieve/remember the right words to complete their thought. Some answer questions with irrelevant and inappropriate answers or with various made-up words (neologisms). So aphasia is an umbrella term to describe a multiplicity of

timeline

300s BC	1864
Plato uses the term to denote speechlessness	Trousseau resurrects the term

language problems. It is possible to list well over a dozen symptoms (e.g. inability to name objects or repeat a phrase, to speak spontaneously or even read), all of which qualify as an accepted symptom of aphasia.

Some people lose their memory specifically for the sound and meaning of words, while others seem to forget how to co-ordinate their tongue and lips to pronounce words properly. They literally cannot 'get their mouths around' certain words.

Early studies of aphasic patients led to the discovery of cerebral dominance: the finding that it is damage to the left (not right) hemisphere that is associated with brain damage. Indeed, aphasia has always excited those brain-mapping psychologists who have tried to map very specific lesion/damage sites in the brain with particular and specific communication problems.

> **Speech is the greatest interest and most distinct achievement of man.**
> N. Wiener, 1950

Locating aphasia Usually, aphasias are a result of damage (lesions) to the language centres of the brain. These areas are almost always located in the left hemisphere, and in most people this is where the ability to produce and comprehend language is found. However, in a very small number of people language ability is found in the right hemisphere. In either case, damage to these language areas can be caused by a stroke or traumatic brain injury. Aphasia may also develop slowly, as in the case of a brain tumour.

Different types of aphasias are caused when brain damage is located in different areas. The two most common are *non-fluent* and *receptive* aphasias, caused when damage is localized to Broca's area or Wernicke's area respectively. Non-fluent aphasia is characterized by slow, laborious, non-fluent speech. From this, psychologists have learnt that Broca's area, in the motor association cortex of the left frontal lobe, is responsible for motor memories: the sequence of muscular movements that is needed to make words. Moreover, damage to Broca's area often produces agrammatism – sufferers cannot comprehend complex syntactical rules (for example, they rarely use function words).

> **I don't want to talk grammar, I want to talk like a lady.**
> G.B. Shaw, *Pygmalion* 1912

1865	1868	2002
First classification	Broca notes brain part responsible for deviant language	Hale, *The Man Who Lost his Language*

Wernicke's area appears to be responsible for the recognition of speech, and receptive aphasia is portrayed by poor speech comprehension and the production of meaningless words. People affected are usually unaware of their disorder as they don't fully and accurately comprehend their own speech. It has been hypothesized that Wernicke's area is where the memories for the sequence of sounds that constitute words are stored.

'Think much, speak little, write less.'

Proverb

One model of language is that incoming language is received by the auditory cortex and sent to Wernicke's area for comprehension. If a response is needed, a message is sent to Broca's area, which then sends messages to the primary motor cortex, which organizes the muscles to articulate a response.

In addition to helping psychologists understand language, work on aphasias was the basis for modern research into the principle of localization – what areas of the brain are used for serving specific functions.

Types of aphasia   Classification is the beginning of science. There is always an attempt when identifying a mental or physical problem to identify subtypes or groups, and the study of aphasia is no exception. Some clinicians believe there are as many forms of aphasia as there are aphasic patients and that it is futile to attempt to classify them. Others are impressed by striking similarities among patients and that certain very specific symptoms are shared by subgroups of patients.

Some taxonomies are based specifically on the speech deficits (semiological), others on mechanisms of the mind, and some on brain seizure location. The best taxonomies seem to be able to clearly and unequivocally classify a third of all cases into one group, leaving two-thirds as mixed.

The first psychological or behavioural classification was between aphasia of the general faculty of language, where it is only speech and not writing that has become impaired. Later there was a distinction between those who were speechless as opposed to those who spoke but with many errors.

There are various types of taxonomies. Associationist taxonomies look at specific linguistic difficulties associated with specific parts of the brain. Selective lesions impair neural networks which affect specific language. So early researchers talked of *motor* aphasia (memories of movement sensations), *sensory* aphasia (memories of auditory sensation to decode articulated speech) and *conduct* aphasia (both of the above).

The associationists have come up with many distinctions and types of aphasia, including subcortical, cortical and transcortical types. Some types have been named after researchers, like Broca's aphasia and Wernicke's aphasia. Other psychologists have distinguished between word deafness and word blindness.

There have been many other taxonomies, some based on specific theories, others on observation. Freud came up with his own three-fold classification while others have tried a more statistical approach, looking at how patients perform on a range of tests. Some are influenced primarily by the linguistic features of speech. However, there remains no agreement in the area.

Therapy Aphasia that interferes with vocal output or speech has come to be known as a speech pathology. Speech pathology was originally considered to be an educational problem but it can lead to adjustment problems, which means psychologists and psychiatrists are interested as well as neurologists who study brain damage. Some speech disorders are purely physical and based on problems with neuromuscular activities. Speech disorders are different from language disorders, which are problems associated with the communication of meaningful symbols and thoughts.

> ‘After some brain shock, a person may be able to speak, but the wrong word often vexatiously comes to his lips, just as if his Broca shelves had been jumbled.’
> **W. Thompson, 1907**

All therapy begins with diagnostic tests that attempt to measure primary language operations like naming, word and sentence completion, reading words and sentences and writing to dictation. Different therapies are offered for different problems. Some neurologists are sceptical of the value of language therapy, given what they see to be the cause of the problem. Others have noticed the evidence of spontaneous recovery; that is, of the total or partial reconstitution of prior language knowledge and skills without any form of therapy. However, there are professional speech pathologists who spend a great deal of time with aphasia patients trying to understand the cause of their problem as well as trying to help them communicate more efficiently.

the condensed idea
The basis of language is revealed when it is disturbed

49 Dyslexia

'Achievement in handling the tasks of reading and writing is obviously one of the most important axes of social differentiation in modern societies.' J. Goody and J. Watt, 1961

Parents and teachers know how much children of the same age seem to differ not only in their tastes and temperament but also in their acquisition of skills. Some appear to have great difficulty with, and lag behind, their same-age peers in various aspects of reading. They appear to be of normal intelligence but can't pick up the skill. Dyslexics soon get into a vicious circle. Reading is slow, strenuous and frustrating. There is no fun in the activity. Even great effort shows little yield so they do it less, shun reading and therefore never keep up with others in acquiring the skill. Hence there are primary systems referring to reading but secondary characteristics associated with low self-esteem and socio-emotional adjustment.

Definition Dyslexia means difficulty with words. The problem has been called word-blindness and specific reading or writing deficit. It is used by professionals to denote significant and persistent reading difficulties. It is centrally concerned with the difficulty in attaining normal reading ability despite good teaching and hard work. Traditional dyslexia is sometimes called *developmental* dyslexia and is about difficulty acquiring the skill. *Acquired* dyslexia usually results from physical trauma leading to reading difficulties after reading was mastered.

In essence the primary problems for the diagnosis are word decoding and spelling, mainly because of a person's word-sounding or phonological system. It is important to ensure that the problem is not due to inadequate educational opportunities, hearing or visual impairment, neurological disorders or major socio-emotional difficulties. Dyslexia is evident when

timeline

1887	1896
Word first used by German ophthalmologist	First description of childhood dyslexia

accurate and fluent word reading and/or spelling develop slowly, incompetently and with great difficulty. Dyslexia tends to run in families and boys are more vulnerable than girls. This certainly seems to suggest that genetic factors may be important.

History

In the early 1960s it was proposed there were three main causes for general reading backwardness: environmental factors such as poor formal education/teaching and home life deprivation; emotional maladjustment; or some organic and constitutional factor.

The common debate among researchers is whether it is meaningful to think of a simple bell-shaped curve or continuum of normal reading ability, with those way above average at the top and poor readers at the bottom. Some insist that is the case and that reading difficulties are not a discrete entity but a linguistic cut-off point on a scale. Others argue it is quite a different cluster or pattern of cognitive skills.

Decoding and comprehension Reading involves two basic processes. The first is to recognize a string of letters and to decipher the code into a word. One has to learn the letters: how they 'sound' and how syllables are formed. This is a slow and laborious job which most frequently results in reading that is instantaneous and automatic.

The second process is more abstract. It makes the text meaningful and connected to experience. It is possible to decode without comprehension: to absent-mindedly read without anything having 'sunk in'. Dyslexics can have very specific difficulties such as how words are spelled (orthography), what words means (semantics), how sentences are formed (syntactics) and how words are built up of roots, prefixes and suffixes (morphology).

Psychologists have devised word-decoding tests so we can measure how good a person is relative to the average. Testees have to decode words and non-words. Research has indicated that the primary problem appears to be with phonological skills. Dyslexics appear to have particular difficulties

1920
First theory of the cause

1949
International Dyslexia Society founded

1967
First suggestion of subgroups

with the sound structure of words and remembering new words, particularly names. They have difficulty repeating complex words and non-words. Another test is the difference a person has in their reading comprehension compared with their listening comprehension.

Subgroups   As with nearly all psychological problems, experts point out that people with the problem are far from a homogeneous lot and frequently fall into recognizable subgroups. This process of delineating subgroups often helps with precise diagnosis and theory building. The problem with making these fine distinctions is getting agreement from experts on the groups and the terminology. The first distinction, proposed in the 1960s, was between auditory dyslexia (problems in differentiating between phonemes and linking/blending them together into a word) and visual dyslexia (difficulty in interpreting, remembering and understanding letters and images of words). Auditory dyslexics have problems with distinguishing letters that sound the same, like b or p; d or t. Visual dyslexics find difficulty identifying words as visual shapes, so 'mad' looks like 'dam', 'tap' like 'pat', etc. They also spell phonologically, writing 'wot' for 'what', 'ruff' for 'rough'.

Later a distinction was made between dysphonic dyslexia (phonological problems); dyseidetic dyslexia (problems in perceiving words as units); and alexia (a mixed type of phonological and visual processing problems). It was thought that around two-thirds were dysphonic, a tenth dyseidetic and a quarter alexic.

It has been found that people adopt different strategies in reading. The phonological strategy codes common letter groups – *ist*, *ough*, *th* – into clusters and then syllables. Those adopting this strategy sound out the words. Others try whole-word or orthographic reading. Hence it has been proposed there is alexia and orthographic alexia or a mix. Children are tested by reading out non-words like 'frin' or 'weg' or 'sper' and non-phonetic words like 'cough' or 'bough'. Still the best way to diagnose a person's reading difficulties is to look very carefully at the processes they use: what they can and can't do easily and correctly.

Self vs professional diagnosis   The diagnosis of dyslexia is unusual as it often appears to bring comfort to many parents and children. Many adults even appear to boast about it, noting that they were not 'diagnosed' correctly and were thought to be lacking in intelligence or some other ability. This is because the labels indicate not low intelligence

Research

Psychologists in this area use all sorts of methods. Some are intense, in-depth case studies of particular individuals. In the comparative method, two large and as far as possible identical groups (in terms of age, IQ, social background) are measured on many tests. Longitudinal studies look at the development of reading problems and difficulties over time. In experimental studies people are tested under particular conditions. Brain-function studies involve live brain-mapping under particular conditions.

(indeed sometimes the opposite) but a very specific functional failing. Every so often serious academic papers question the very existence of dyslexia, which usually provokes an outcry from affronted reading-disability researchers. Defenders point out that dyslexics are different from poor readers because of their peculiar and specific errors in reading or spelling, despite evidence of normal if not high intelligence and in spite of conventional teaching.

Critics say it is a middle-class condition where affluent parents can't or won't face the fact that their children are not very bright and they attempt to manipulate the education system to their advantage. Others regard this attack as damaging, hurtful and deeply unjustified and possibly related to certain parents expecting far too much of their children.

A central issue is the relationship between dyslexia and IQ. There seems to be a wide belief in the existence of the very bright dyslexic who gets mislabelled as dim, lazy, inattentive or maladjustive. A key notion for dyslexia is that of an unexpectedly poor level of reading in comparison with the ability to learn other skills. There is a discrepancy between ability on reading tests compared with many other subtests of IQ.

> **English orthography is archaic, cumbrous and ineffective: its acquisition consumes much time and effort: failure to acquire it is easy to detect.**
>
> **Thorstein Veblen, 1899**

the condensed idea
There are many types of dyslexia

50 Who's that?

Have you ever been mistaken for somebody else who, in your view, really does not look at all like you? How often do you 'know you know' a person but can't put a name to the face? You know they are a long-distance runner or politician but simply can't access their name. Equally, a face may be very familiar but you can't say much about the person at all.

People say that they 'never forget a face': but self-evidently they do so all the time. Researchers have shown that there is no relationship between how people think they will do in studies of face recognition and how they really do. There is some evidence that people who remember faces better than others simply have a better visual memory. That is, they have a better-than-average ability to remember paintings, maps and written scripts. They seem to have a special facility with pictures and images.

> **Face and facial expression define our uniqueness and individuality and act to conceal as well as reveal.**
>
> **J. Cole, 1977**

Prosopagnosia The ability to recognize and identify people is of fundamental importance in everyday life. Imagine not being able to recognize your partner in a crowd, or failing to identify your parents at a party or your boss in the office. The importance of memory for faces is most dramatically seen in a problem called *prosopagnosia*. People with this problem cannot recognize familiar faces – even, on occasions, their own in a mirror. Surprisingly, many prosopagnosic patients can relatively easily distinguish between other similar objects – cars, books and even types of spectacles – but not faces.

A central question for psychology is whether there are special and specific face-processing mechanisms different from the identification of other objects. This would require identifying and investigating two very special

timeline

1510	18th–19th centuries
Leonardo da Vinci sketches various nose shapes	High point of caricaturists and cartoonists

> Men with small foreheads are fickle, whereas if they are rounded or bulging out the owners are quick tempered. Straight eyebrows indicate softness of disposition, those that curve out toward the temples, humour and dissimulation. The staring eye indicates impudence, and winking indecision. Large and outstanding ears indicate a tendency to irrelevant talk or chattering.
>
> **Aristotle, 350 BC**

and (thankfully) rare types of people: those who have normal face recognition but poor object recognition (*visual agnosia*) and the opposite, which is the problem of prosopagnosia. The question for cognition neuropsychologists is whether we can identify separate brain regions and mechanisms that are dedicated to and responsible for face recognition and object recognition.

Certainly evidence to date on brain-damaged and non brain-damaged patients with prosopagnosia does suggest there are very specific brain regions (the mid-fusiform gyrus and occipital gyrus) which may be responsible for face processing.

The whole and its parts A two-process model has been suggested to differentiate between face and object recognition. One process is called *holistic analysis*, which involves the processing of the 'big picture': total configuration, overall structure. This is contrasted with the *analysis by parts*, which focuses on the details and then attempts to put them together. The idea is that face recognition involves a much more holistic analysis than object recognition.

This can be very well demonstrated with photo-fit technology. In the 1970s the photo-fit system was devised that involved a person 'constructing a face' from a wide range of parts. Thus there was a large range of noses representing all the common shapes. The same was applied to mouth, eyes and hair, etc. This led to a large number of experiments to test accuracy. Could

1971
Photo-fit system introduced

1976
Lord Devlin argues unsupported eyewitness facial recognition too unreliable to convict

1988
V. Bruce, *Recognising Faces*

"Minds differ more than faces."

Voltaire, 1750

people construct a good, recognizable picture of their partner; a famous politician; even themselves? To do this they would have to know, and choose a particular shape, of mouth, eyes, etc. The results showed how poor people were at this task of deriving an overall pattern from the pieces.

Studies have also shown how disguising one aspect of a person easily leads to a dramatic drop in recognition. The addition of a wig, a beard or glasses causes a significant drop in facial recognition, as criminals have long known. Even showing people a profile or three-quarters of a face rather than a 'full frontal' has a dramatic effect. It seems that people process the whole face/pattern in one go, not in parts. Further, they seem to process faces in terms of personality characteristics. Hence people talk of an honest face, rugged good looks, delicate or dodgy. Consider how you would describe the face of Winston Churchill or Nelson Mandela. Do you do so in terms of the size of their mouth or shape of their eyes? Generally not.

Many interesting studies in this area have involved producing distorted pictures. Some involve configural distortions, involving moving the eyes and mouth around, perhaps even inverting the whole face. Others involve component distortions, which consist of distorting one component like blackening of the teeth. Studies have found that component distortions are

Factors influencing the process

There are some interesting results from studies on this process, some more commonsensical than others.

- The longer you see a face, the more easily it is recognized.

- The less similar the face to the witness's, the less it is recognized.

- Face recognition does not decay much over time: the passage of time has a minimal effect.

- It does not matter much if a person sees another 'live', on video or in a photograph – recognition is about the same.

- Upside-down photographs are disproportionately difficult to recognize.

- If a face is 'distinctive' (unusual, untypical), it is easier to recognize.

nearly always detected, but that is not true of configural distortions. It has therefore been assumed that prosopagnosia involves impaired holistic or configural processing while visual agnosia involves impaired holistic and analytic processing.

Components of the process To understand the complex process of face recognition, psychologists have suggested that there are separate components that work together to produce the overall system. These include such skills as *expression analysis*, which is the ability to infer internal emotional states from facial features and expressions. Next there is *facial speech analysis*, which is the ability to 'lip read' to better understand speech. There is of course direct *visual processing*, which is the ability to process selected aspects of the face, especially eye expressions, and distinct facial expressions. Another is *face recognition units*, which contain information about the structure (long, round, sad) of faces known to the person.

In addition there are *name generation processes*, which show we store (in memory) a person's name as well as *person identity nodes*, which help a person store details about specific individuals – their age, hobbies, job and so on. Finally there is a *general cognitive* or *knowledge* system, which is a store of knowledge about people (for example, athletes tend to be fit, actresses attractive, alcoholics ruddy-faced, etc.).

A breakdown in any one system influences the whole process. The components that seem most important for everyday facial recognition are:

- the structural encoding: logging in memory what people notice in a particular face and their unique nodes, and
- name generation.

Facial recognition is an important, active area of applied psychological research that is becoming all the more important in the security world. Indeed, to teach computers to recognize and remember people is the most obvious application of this whole research enterprise.

> **'Your face, my thane, is as a book where men May read strange matters.'**
> **Shakespeare, *Macbeth* 1606**

the condensed idea
Memory for faces tells us much about how the brain works

Glossary

ADHD Attention-Deficit Hyperactivity Disorder associated with attention difficulties in concentrating, listening to others, following instructions, impulsivity and constant fidgeting.

anxiety disorders A range of related problems all characterised by angst, anxiety, and stress reactions which include panic attacks; phobias of all sorts; acute, generalised and post-traumatic stress disorder; substance induced anxiety.

aphasia A disorder of speech (language production) usually caused by cortical lesions. It may reveal itself as an inability to use or produce speech clearly or accurately or understand speech of others.

behaviourism A theory that emphasises the pre-eminence of observable behaviour as a criterion for study and emphasises the role of the social environment in deteremining most human behaviour.

bell curve Also know as the normal distribution. This is a plot of the scores of many people that results in a bell shape with most people scoring on and around the middle/average and relatively few at either extreme.

California F scale A measure of fascist beliefs and attitudes devised over 50 years ago by a group of sociologists trying to understand authoritarianism and the origin of Nazism.

classical conditioning A type of learning where a neutral stimulus called the conditioned stimulus is paired with the unconditioned stimulus.

cognitive behaviour therapy (CBT) A modern and very popular 'talking cure' that focuses on trying to change how people think about, attribute or perceive things that happen to them.

cognitive dissonance A self-perceived and uncomfortable inconsistency or incongruency between attitudes, beliefs, experiences or feelings.

delusion A false persistent opinion or belief that is both insubstantiable and not open to reasonable change often concerning ideas about being followed, loved, deceived, infected or poisoned.

dyslexia A complex and still disputed disorder specifically of reading ability.

ego The rational, reality principle, conscious part of the self. Sometimes thought of as the general manager of personality and rational decision-making that mediates between the selfish *id* and the moral *superego*.

electro-convulsive therapy (ECT) A somatic psychiatric treatment used mainly for chronic depression involving a brief, but strong , electric current that is passed through the brain to produce a short, convulsive seizure.

emotional intelligence (EI) Being perceptive and highly aware of the emotional state of oneself as well as others, and the ability to manage or change one's own or others' emotional state.

emotional intelligence quotient (EQ) A score like the intelligence quotient (IQ) that is a comparative, reliable and valid measure of a person's emotional intelligence.

Flynn effect Evidence that IQ scores of the population of many countries is rising.

gestalt An integrated whole that is more than the summation of its parts. A configuration, form, pattern or structure or visual, or audio stimuli.

heuristics A rule of thumb, procedure or formula that has worked in the past and may guide problem-solving in the future.

id Unconscious instinctual demands (libido and psychic energy) particularly around sex and violence that operate exclusively by the pleasure principle.

intelligence quotient (IQ) A ratio measure that reflects whether a person's mental age (MA) is ahead of or behind their chronological age (CA).

mood disorders These include depressive disorders characterised by depressed mood, inactivity, insomnia, fatigue, weight-loss, feelings of worth-lessness and guilt; and bipolar disorder characterised by alternating depressive and manic phases.

multiple intelligence The idea, not supported by evidence, that there are various independent and unrelated mental capacities.

obsessive-compulsive disorder (OCD) A disorder characterised by excessive, unreasonable yet recurrent and persistent thoughts, impulses and images as well as repetitive behaviours.

operant conditioning (*or* instrumental conditioning) A form of learning where a reinforcer (food, praise, money, etc.) is given exclusively after a person or animal performs a very specific act.

paranoid personality disorder Pervasive distrust and suspiciousness of other people's behaviours and motives which are always interpreted as malevolent.

phrenology A now largely defunct 'science' of the brain and mind that believed the skull revealed accurately the structure of each individual's brain.

placebo A medically or chemically inert substance or procedure that a person (usually patient but also practitioner) believes will help them or make them recover and which is used in scientific research to determine real treatment efficacy.

polygraph An apparatus commonly referred to as a lie detector which measures various physiological responses to questions.

psychopath A person with a persistent pattern of total and guiltless disregard for, and violation of, the rights and feelings of other people.

psychopathology The study of a wide rage of psychological disorders.

psychosis A broad category of serious psychological disorders that imply a loss of normal mental functioning and where a person's thoughts and behaviours are clearly out of touch with reality.

REM sleep Rapid Eye Movement, or active sleep which is a stage of sleep where people appear to dream and where brain activity is very similar to that which occurs when people are awake.

S-curve A particularly shaped curve technically called the sigmoid curve which shows an S shape: the initial growth is first steeply exponential, then it flattens, saturation occurs and the 'growth' stops. The curve has interesting statistical properties.

schema An organising mental framework or knowledge structure that serves to categorise and synthesise information about people, places or things.

schizophrenia A disorder characterised by delusions, hallucinations, disorganised speech and behaviour and flat emotions as well as social and occupational dysfunction.

sociopath Another word for psychopath or one experiencing an antisocial personality disorder.

spatial intelligence The ability to think visually in geometric forms and comprehend pictorial representations of solid objects and to recognise the relationships resulting from movements of objects in space.

stress A complex behavioural, cognitive and physiology reaction of an individual to some real or imagined situation (stimulus, person, event) that is felt to endanger or threaten well-being.

substance disorders Substance dependence which is characterised by tolerance (an increasing dosage required for similar effects), withdrawal symptoms, great effort put into obtaining the substance, a reduction of social, occupational and recreational activities and unsuccessful efforts to cut down on consumption.

superego The repository of a person's moral values and being and made up of the conscience which is the moral rules, sanctions and requirements of society and *ego* ideals which are the individual and idiosyncratic internalization of personal goals.

tabula rasa Literally a blank slate of tablet used to describe the young infant mind before it is written upon by experience.

verbal reasoning A mental faculty that concerns the specific ability to understand the meaning of words and ideas associated with them and to present ideas and information clearly to others.

Index

Dedication
For Alison and Benedict who are always
full of good ideas . . . mainly about reforming me.

Quercus Publishing Plc
21 Bloomsbury Square
London WC1A 2NS

First published in 2008

A catalogue record of this book is available from the British Library

ISBNs
Cloth case edition   ISBN-13: 978 1 84724 852 7
Printed case edition ISBN-13: 978 1 84724 656 1

Printed and bound in China

10 9 8 7 6 5 4 3 2 1

Prepared by *specialist* publishing services ltd, Montgomery